HINDUSTAN'S HORIZONS

HINDUSTAN'S HORIZONS

Brenton Thoburn Badley

GYAN

Published by

Gyan Publishing House
5, Ansari Road
Daryaganj, New Delhi-110002
Phone: 011-47034999, 9811692060
E-mail: books@gyanbooks.com

Distribution Network
gyanbooks.com
India, USA, Canada, UK, Australia, France

ISBN: 978-81-212-8624-4 (PB)
First Published, 1923

2nd Impression 2023

Printed at: Gyan Press, Delhi.

HINDUSTAN'S HORIZONS
Author: Brenton Thoburn Badley

Photo by B. T. Badley.

India's face is towards the light. There is a great day ahead, and those who really know her realise that her "tide" is "at the flood." NOW is the great word in India to-day.

HINDUSTAN'S HORIZONS

By

Brenton Thoburn Badley

Executive Office:

THE CENTENARY FORWARD MOVEMENT
OF INDIA AND BURMA
Calcutta, India

Dedicated to

MRS. LOIS S. PARKER,

Since 1859 a missionary to India,
bringing America's best to India's need,
filling each of the sixty-four years
with ceaseless toil and fervent love
for Hindustan's people,
and ever walking in white before them,

AN EXEMPLAR OF
THE HIGHEST LIFE AND
TRUEST SERVICE.

TO THE READER OF THIS BOOK.

SOME things stand out to-day with startling boldness on Hindustan's wide horizons. It is only with these that this little book is concerned.

For the first time surveys of the Episcopal Areas by our Resident Bishops are published. They will help the purpose of this book, namely to interpret for those who watch India from afar the things of outstanding significance for the Kingdom of God. This little volume will serve also to bring up to date the record of the Methodist Centenary Forward Movement in India.

For the beautiful cover-design we are indebted to Mrs. H. A. Hanson of Sitapur.

The far horizons of Hindustan have a great and growing significance for our world. Another generation will understand more fully what ours has begun to comprehend,—that human history and human destiny are closely bound up with the three hundred and nineteen millions of our race who live in India. For on Hindustan's horizon to-day the greatest figure is the Majestic Christ.

3, Middleton Street,
Calcutta.

POLITICS AND RELIGION IN MODERN HINDUSTAN.

HINDUSTAN to-day is on the world's horizon. A country as old as Egypt is showing signs of youth that place her among the most modern lands.

India's political sky is being scanned by the leaders of the world. What is happening here is of international significance because for the first time since the West came in contact with the East India is politically awake. And when one-fifth of the world's inhabitants wake up after centuries of sleep, the world itself must become a different place. India's weight in the scales of the world, whether intellectually, commercially, politically or spiritually, must materially determine the world's condition.

The outstanding fact regarding India to-day is that a *people* are in the process of becoming a *nation*. This is, of necessity, a complex process, for India not only has as many and as distinct races as Europe, but has a larger population than that continent.

A National Character,—at last!

For the first time since Europe touched India, a truly national character has arisen. Never before in the history of modern India has any man become universally known. To-day, Gandhi's name is on all lips from Cape Comorin to

Photo by B. T. Badley.

The horizon never ends on India's broad plains. Under these bright skies is being worked out the destiny of one-fifth of our race.

Peshawar and from Karachi to Rangoon. This is not because his idea and plan of "Non-co-operation" with the British Government has met the approval of all his fellow countrymen, but because he has incarnated the new spirit of *Young India*, seeking to realise herself and find her own place in the modern world. Gandhi has awakened the national spirit from end to end in a land so vast and filled with such a variety of people, speaking so many languages, that nothing else ever has stirred them all.

Gandhi is in prison as a seditionist and as one openly seeking to make impossible the existing

Photo by E. M. Moffatt.

A Hindu temple whose top is covered with pieces of tin made from the Standard Oil Company's tins. The possibilities of " reform " are almost unlimited!

government, but the influence of his life and his spirit abides. Could he have seen his way to co-operate with the Government and by constitutional means to bring about the self-determination for which India's leaders strive, as others of his

Photo by B. T. Badley.

Modern methods are penetrating even far into the Himalayah mountains. These "Sandwich" men, representing the "Red Lamp" cigarettes, were found on the job four marches up in the interior.

countrymen are doing, he might still have been working out India's destiny. Gandhi was not more patriotic than Rabindranath Tagore, Srinivasa Shastri, K. Natarajan, and scores of other famous Indians who saw no hope or wisdom in non-co-operation, but his eager spirit could not brook the delays that are necessary in a land where the great majority of people are not only ignorant and backward but without a political consciousness or any experience of national movements. With no national citizenship achieved, India cannot meet the demands or rise to the duties and responsibilities of Home Rule. Wiser heads than Gandhi's saw that to force complete self-government on India before her people were ready for it, was the surest way to wreck all the hopes of the future.

Photo by B. T. Badley.

This Hindu "holy man" has loaded himself with chains in order to "mortify" his flesh. He is typical of India. groaning under many self-imposed disabilities.

Yet far more rapidly than could ever have been anticipated by the most ardent of India's admirers, is a national consciousness and a common citizenship coming into existence. Were it not for the most delicate and difficult problems that Hindu-Moslem rivalries, jealousies and antipathies bring upon this land, a national unity would be well assured. But the solution of this problem,

Photo by M. T. Titus.

A Mohommedan "Sufi" or mystic.

Photo by B. T. Badley.

American products are penetrating far into India's interior. This shows a village of Bengal where Mobiloils are advertised.

despite the assurances of enthusiasts and idealists, is still ahead. Dr. Ansari, a leader in the Mohommedan political camp, has just stated that in comparison with the need of securing Hindu-Moslem unity, all other public questions in India are as nothing. In view of the riots that have recently broken out, and the strained relations that exist, this statement is not too strong. Whether Hindus and Mohommedans can ever really pull together in India is still an open question. Politicians say—" We have a pact and unity is assured." The man in the bazaar says—" Oil and water will not mix!" For the present, a system of separate communal representation in the government is, after a fashion, meeting the practical difficulty, but it does not promise much as a permanent arrangement.

A Solution Offered by Christ.

After all, the true solution of India's problems, political, social and spiritual, can be found only in Christianity. Not only would the acceptance of Christ give these people a real unity, but His personality and principles would guarantee the moral force that is essential if India is ever to have good government of her own. Neither Hinduism nor Islam can produce the moral and spiritual fibre that must enter into a safe and stable national life. The principles of Christ are indispensable. This a few of the most thoughtful and spiritually minded of India's leaders seem to recognize. They are speaking the language of the new day. Rabindranath Tagore refuses to let an idol be brought on the premises of his great new University. Gandhi urges every Hindu to become "a close student of the Bible." The Editor of the "Indian Social Reformer" calls upon missionaries to "stand by India in her endeavour to apply the central teachings of Christ to her national life." Sir Ashutosh Mukerji, late Vice-Chancellor of the Calcutta University, declares in a great public meeting, "The Bible has been the greatest influence in my life." Sir Narayan Chandarvarkar, one of Bombay's greatest Hindu leaders whose recent death India mourns, put himself on record thus :—

> "India is being converted: the ideas that lie at the heart of the Gospel are slowly but surely permeating every part of Hindu society, and modifying every phase of Hindu thought."

Photo by B. T. Badley.

India needs fewer dreamers on the banks of the Ganges and more workers at the unending tasks in every department of her new life. Her need is not more religion but more spiritual life,—a practical application of the principles of Christ to her every-day affairs.

The Maharajah of Travancore says :—

" It is the Christian's Bible that will, sooner or later, work out the regeneration of India."

Even Buddhism is seeking to-day to revivify its antiquarian religion by linking up Christ with Buddha. Take the following extracts from a recent article in " The World and the New Dispensation " (Calcutta) :—

" So is Buddha's personality alive and throbbing and marching on—a figure of world importance and divine proportions ! He is out to conquer and to leaven all. What purpose will it serve to-day to predicate life and immortality to Christ, and at the same time fail to see Buddha alive and active? This is a negation of God,—a kind of atheism of

Photo by B. T. Badley.

The missionary car, whether it brings tracts, medicines or the Christian message, always has a " following " in the rural areas.

a subtle and deadly type. No, Buddha is not dead, nor in the 'past tense', nor a mere 'memory.' He is an exile even as Christ is from much that is called Christian in the civilised world to-day. Behold Buddha and Christ are together,—these fellow-exiles. They are members one of another in some subtle and mysterious way, organically bound up with one another and with all humanity in the present consciousness of God."

Photo by B. T. Badley.

A deputation of "Untouchables" (tanners and leather dressers) coming to an Indian district superintendent and his council to ask for spiritual instruction for their people. Such requests sometimes involve thousands of souls.

This turning to Christ is a first step towards accepting Christianity, and is probably the most striking thing on India's horizon to-day. Indeed, the political and social awakening of India is a direct result of the spread of influences that are traceable to Christ's Gospel. The dynamic of

Christ's teachings and the power of His personality are the greatest factors in shaping modern India. The greatest school of the nations is Hindustan and her greatest teacher is the living Christ. To His words India is attending as possibly no other non-Christian land of the world. Yet it cannot be denied that there is a marked revival of both Hinduism and Mohommedanism in India. These communities were never more alert and aggressive than to-day. But one must look deeper than the formalities of religion or the activities that appear on the surface, to get a true understanding of the trend of events. Earnest men, Hindus and Mohommedans, spending themselves for a land in the making, find themselves unable to supply for these vast multitudes the purity and power that come only from the abiding Christ.

Photo by B. T. Badley.

A devotee of the goddess Kali, bowing over the sacrificial posts in front of the temple at Kalighat.

Photo by L. A. Core.

A Hindu "holy" man, swinging head down over a fire of dried cow-dung cakes. Foolish? Yes,—but also another indication of India's wealth of devotion to religion.

Photo by B. T. Badley.

A licensed liquor shop in one of Calcutta's busiest thoroughfares. In such places foreign spirits are increasingly in demand by Indian drinkers.

India's Reformers Make Discoveries.

Reformers who, seeing what Christian Missions have accomplished in elevating the depressed classes and building character of integrity and unselfishness where Islam and Hinduism through the centuries had failed to lift or empower, have adopted the message and methods of the missionary and entered hopefully on the supreme task of making men and women of integrity, purity, intelligence and patriotism. To their amazement they are discovering two remarkable things. First, that they are standing shoulder to shoulder with the missionary. They had thought he was some sort of proselytizing agent, not primarily concerned with the task of making better citizens. They imagined that he was living and working in a realm of creeds and ideals, but find him toiling patiently at the practical things that enter into everyday life and work. It is dawning on the consciousness of India's non-Christian leaders that Christian missionaries saw a hundred years ago what the nationalist " reformers " have just comprehended, *viz.*, that you cannot have a better India until you have men and women purer and truer and more unselfish, saved from the blights of sordid social cults and freed from the fetters of degraded religious systems. Modern India, they begin to

Photo by B. T. Badley.

A licensed shop for the sale of "toddy," the fermented liquor of the palm tree. This large shed accommodates scores of people. Liquor and lives are cheap in India!

Those who participated in the inter-communal dinner at Bombay. This group includes Europeans and Indians, high caste and low caste, Hindus and Christians, Parsis and Mohommedans, men and women,—marking a new era in the social reform movement.

comprehend, demands not that the religion or traditions of the fore-fathers be preserved, but that people through their religion and customs be fitted to enter upon the practical duties of citizenship. Social service, they begin to understand, has its foundations on a true, spiritual life. Already India's non-Christian leaders have realised that the "outcaste" millions must be lifted out of their

Photo by B. T. Badley.

In a north India poppy field. The man with a knife is scraping the juice that has exuded from the slit made the night before on the pod.

degradation if India's people are to prosper. In some cases far-seeing men in the Hindu camp have realised that from these very " depressed " classes may come the forces that will save Hindu society itself. The Editor of the " Indian Social Reformer " has just said editorially in his paper—" The salvation of the country, it is becoming increasingly clear, will come mainly from the depressed and repressed sections of the Indian people,—Sudras and women." Then he quotes the Bible as if it were his own book,—" The stone which the builders had set at naught will become the head of the corner."

Photo by E. M. Moffatt.

A Hindu boy ascetic: his body is smeared with ashes. This ancient Hindu method of training leaders does not find much favour in India's new day.

Photo by B. T. Badley.

Spinning has received an impetus recently in India, but it can do little to solve the economic problem that is now being faced.

The Pathetic Position of "Reformers."

But a more amazing discovery than this is being made by India's reformers. It is this, that they are without the power to make people better! They had supposed that if ignorant people were enlightened, they would become good. Their idea had been that if the upward way was pointed out to men they would arise and tread it. They had imagined that if a community were given correct teaching, right living would follow. To raise the depressed, you had only to show the way up: to reform the drunkard, it was only necessary to make clear to him that the community needed in him a pure, strong life: to make a patriot, the task was really to enlighten him as to the need of the motherland in the hour of opportunity. But to the surprise and confusion of the " reformer " human nature with its selfishness, pride, sensuality, love of ease and all the failings of the unregenerate heart refuses to yield to his exhortations. His strenuous public utterances are applauded, his vigorous writings are read and fully approved, but men and women go home to live the same sordid lives as before. He is an acknowledged " reformer," but he does not know how to re-form people. There is nothing more pathetic in India to-day.

What can the " Reformer " do? What can the patriot further propose? The fact is that only Christ can re-form lives. Only He who said " Ye must be born again " can bring man to the new life, where the individual becomes in and through Christ a " New Creation," with a desire for the higher, a love of the purer, a willingness, even eagerness, to sacrifice for others, and a power to live the expanding, fruitful life. The truth of this is slowly dawning on the consciousness of India's patriots and reformers. This realization is the forerunner of a new day.

On India's spiritual horizon the majestic Christ is supreme.

THE CHURCH IN A NEW INDIA.

CLEARER than ever before is the significance of the Centenary Forward Movement in India to-day. Here, as elsewhere, the break-up of the old world marks the beginning of the new. This period of transition has been a time of unexampled activity. Events have moved with amazing rapidity since the close of the war, and perhaps India has taken larger strides forward during these few years than any other land. Greater problems, political, social and moral, have been faced by India since 1918 than at any time previous. Larger adjustments have been brought about than anyone thought possible. More far-reaching decisions have been made than in any preceding period.

The re-actions of the great war have come up against India with great shocks. Economic difficulties have beset her just when she was in the greatest political ferment. Social revolutions have come upon her before she could adjust herself to the changing conditions resulting from her entry upon an international career. Failing markets in Europe and fluctuating exchange rates have struck her just when the temporary boom following the close of the war subsided, leaving her in serious financial straits.

Methodism's Morale in India.

All this rendered still more difficult the work of foreign missions in India. It is the more apparent when we recall that this was for India also the period of failing faith in the Christian lands and civilisation of the West, and an overweening confidence in self. Christianity was supposed to have borne its legitimate fruit in the unparalleled destruction of the great war and its untold cruelties and sufferings. For India, the war virtually wiped Europe off the map; nor has anything that has happened there since the Peace Treaty was signed changed her thought about that continent. Non-Christians had their confidence seriously shaken and Christians had fresh disappointments to face.

Failing finances in Europe and England coincided with failing morale in India, with the result that considerable sections of the work of Missionary Societies of Churches of those lands have had to

Photo by H. H. Weak.

A "Centenary" school in the Pauri district, situated more than a mile above sea level.

be given up. Schools and colleges have been closed, fields of labor abandoned and workers dismissed. This has led to such reverses as to alarm the Indian constituencies of those Churches and has resulted in unstable conditions.

Now it is a remarkable fact that during this very period, 1918-1923, the Methodist Episcopal Church in India has made some of her greatest advances. This period of the Centenary affords a

Photo by L. Chester Lewis.

"Girl Guides" of the Girls' High School, Cawnpore, out on an "elephant picnic."

most encouraging survey of the work of our Church in India. Nothing less than such a real "forward movement" as the Centenary enterprise represents could have saved the Methodist Episcopal Church from just such serious reverses as have been experienced during this period by other Missions in this land.

There were two main factors that contributed

Photo by S. Aldis.

The missionary's ox-cart crossing a river of the Central Provinces,—all in the day's work.

to our continued success. First, there was the most heartening realization that the Church at the Home Base had both the intention and ability to continue and even increase its appropriations to the foreign field. While all these hopes were not realised, yet the financial giving was kept at a level that enabled the Methodist Episcopal Church in India to tide over this unusually difficult period. Had the funds from America failed at this time, not only would the work of our Church in India have suffered a great reverse, but her morale might have been seriously impaired.

The other factor that saved the situation was that the enthusiasm generated by the compelling call for a great forward movement on the part of the Church in India itself, kept our people from yielding to the sag that has undoubtedly marked the years 1921-1923.

Photo by B. T. Badley.

Whether it be a "Dodge," an "Overland," or only a "Ford," rural Bengal (barring the roads!) is a paradise for the motor,—and its occupants. Better roads follow rather than precede motor traffic.

Several considerations made this depression specially marked in India. (1) There was what has already been indicated, a serious economic and financial disturbance following the post-war adjustments. (2) The Church had to face the waning confidence of India's people in Western civilization and the Christianity of Europe, and re-interpret the essentials of the Gospel in the terms of India's new life and needs. (3) The social ferment throughout the land has brought disturbing problems to the front. (4) The unprecedented political unrest throughout the country has unduly drawn the attention of the people to purely secular things and over-emphasized political

Photo by B. T. Badley.

Primary education is one of the supreme needs of India. We can get along without buildings, but not without the teachers.

Photo by M. T. Titus.

The family "automobile" in north India on the way to a "mela" or religious fair.

matters. (5) In some parts of the land Indian Christians have been persecuted as unpatriotic, because they would not lend their support to the ultra-radical and revolutionary propaganda with which the extremist agitators sought to overthrow the existing government. It was a severe handicap, indeed, when a considerable section of India's people thought our Christians unpatriotic. This misunderstanding is gradually clearing up.

Under all these disadvantages success could come only if the morale of the Church were unimpaired, her faith and vision maintained and her zeal, enthusiasm and devotion kept alive. No mere "statesmanship" could have brought this about. A mere knowledge of what the situation demanded could not avail. The need was for a mighty motive, a dominating determination, a compelling conviction that would carry the membership of the Church over the obstacles and through to the larger fields of endeavour. This is precisely what the Centenary Movement furnished in India. So outstanding has been the service thus rendered by this Movement in India to Methodism here, and so direct has been the bearing of the Movement at the Home Base on the present strength and efficiency of our India work, that we need not leave it to historians of future decades to point out the significance of the Centenary Forward Movement to the Methodist Episcopal Church in India.

The leaders of Methodism in India know how the Centenary saved the day. In India we have had not merely a movement within the Church,—the whole Church has been moving.

Photo by F. Wood.

Old "Grant Road" Church in Bombay being re-built to meet modern conditions: now known as "Centenary" Church,—one of our notable Centenary undertakings in India.

Photo by B. T. Badley.

The new "Gracey Memorial Church" at Sitapur, United Provinces,—another Centenary project splendidly completed.

Raising Rupees during Slumps and Sags.

Perhaps the most notable success achieved by the Methodist Episcopal Church in India during this period was in just the line of effort where it was least expected, *viz.*, the financial. At a time of national unrest, trade depression and unstable conditions in all departments, a decreased amount raised on this field would not have been surprising and would have been pardoned. But our Church in India demonstrated a vitality and showed a spiritual power that have greatly increased her self-respect and we trust have strengthened the faith of

Photo by L. A. Core.

A typical village scene.

our friends at the Home Base. These facts are noted here for the encouragement of the Church at the Home Base whose courage and sacrifice Indian Methodism so fully appreciates, and also to show the patrons of this great work how worthily Indian Methodism has responded to their continued confidence and support.

During the first three of the Centenary years in India, *i.e.*, 1919-1921, the yearly giving of Methodists in India rose by the amount of $97,980, which represents an increase of seventy-three per cent. During this period an amount of $365,193 was raised on this field and added to what was appropriated to India by our Board of Foreign Missions. The significance of this cannot be grasped until we realise that the average income of a family in the rural areas of India comes to about $4.50 a month. This is not a "living wage" on any decent plane of life, but to tens of thousands of people in their mud huts, we must go and get the pittance that they can give by foregoing something additional in their meagre lives. The " tens of thousands " are not a figure of speech. At least ninety per cent. of our membership in Indian Methodism are to be found in the villages. This means that somewhat more than 360,000 of our Indian Methodists are included in this class. If the Methodists of the United States of America should give at this same rate in proportion to their income, not only could the entire Centenary programme be easily financed, but the total requirements of the ill-fated Inter-Church Movement could have been largely met by our Methodism alone.

Photo by B. T. Badley.

Just girls, at the entrance to a Hindu temple: another ten years, and then——?

It will be of interest to compare the total amounts raised on this field during the past four quadrenniums,—1911-1923. The figures for the first three quadrenniums are as follows :—

Total for quadrennium ending	1911	Rs. 1,520,503
,, ,, ,,	1915	Rs. 1,708,077
,, ,, ,,	1919	Rs. 2,691,546

The increase of nearly one million Rupees in 1919 shows the impetus given by the Centenary. The figures for 1923 cannot be had until the end of this year. If due allowance is made for Malaysia and the Philippine Islands having been taken from the Southern Asia field in 1920, and if the 73 per cent. increase registered in 1919-1921* should be maintained to the end of the present quadrennium, the total amount raised in India during the current quadrennium should give us another increase of one million Rupees.

Considering that this quadrennium includes the " financial slump " period, such a result should hearten not only India but world-wide Methodism.

Sixty Millions moving Christ-wards.

Our Methodism in Hindustan is more concerned, however, as to souls saved than rupees raised.

No foreign mission field of the world has afforded so many accessions to the Church as has India. This field was not entered by American Methodism till 1856, and is thus one of the youngest among our major fields of effort.

When the " Central Conference " of India was organized in 1885 (and subsequently put into the " Discipline " of our Church through the efforts of our India missionaries), the total Christian

* NOTE —These figures have just been published through our Board of Foreign Missions at New York.

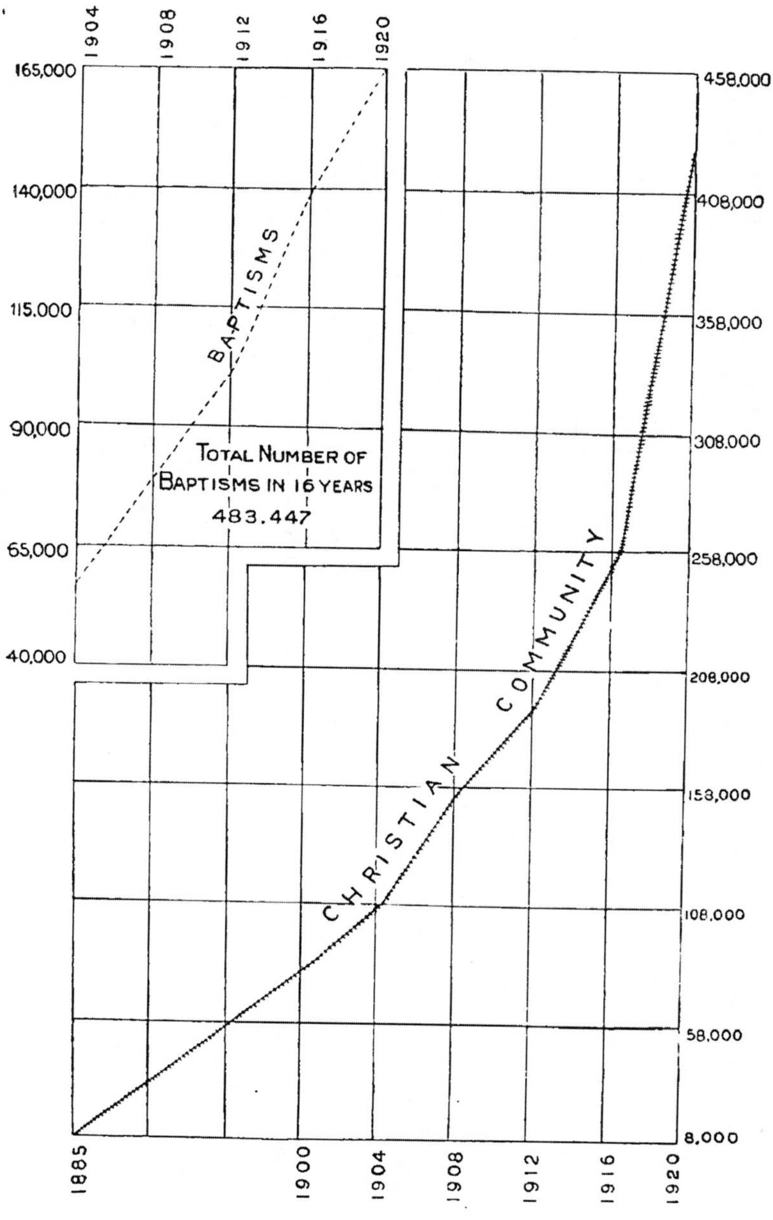
Total Number of
Baptisms in 16 years
483.447
BAPTISMS
CHRISTIAN COMMUNITY
165,000
140,000
115,000
90,000
65,000
40,000
458,000
408,000
358,000
308,000
258,000
208,000
158,000
108,000
58,000
8,000
1904
1908
1912
1916
1920
1885
1900
1904
1908
1912
1916
1920

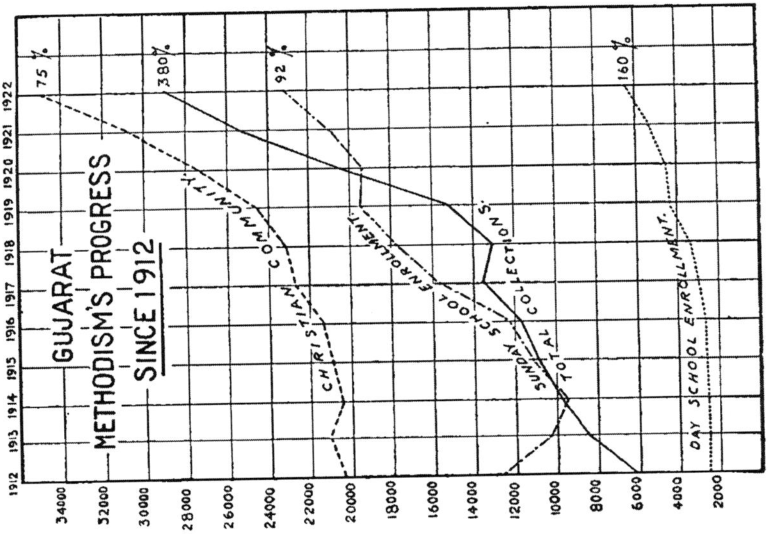
GUJARAT
METHODISM'S PROGRESS
SINCE 1912
CHRISTIAN COMMUNITY
SUNDAY SCHOOL ENROLLMENT
TOTAL COLLECTIONS
DAY SCHOOL ENROLLMENT
75 %
380 %
92 %
160 %

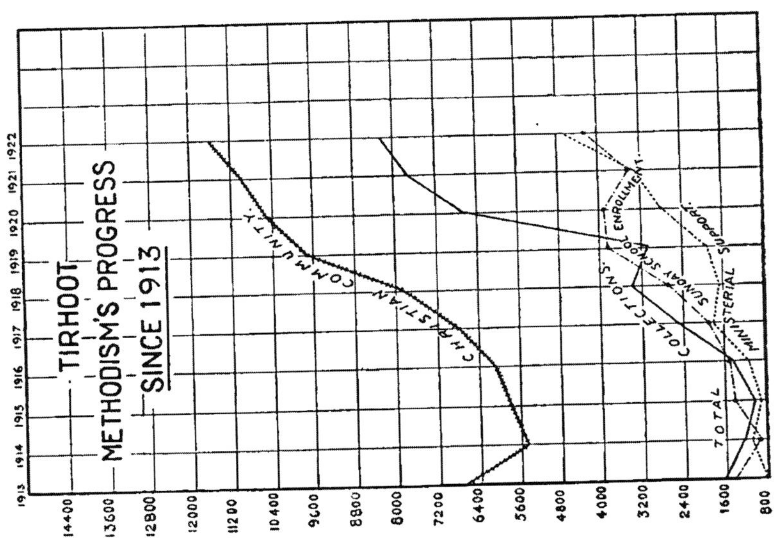
TIRHOOT
METHODISM'S PROGRESS
SINCE 1913
CHRISTIAN COMMUNITY
SUNDAY SCHOOL ENROLLMENT
COLLECTIONS
TOTAL MINISTERIAL SUPPORT

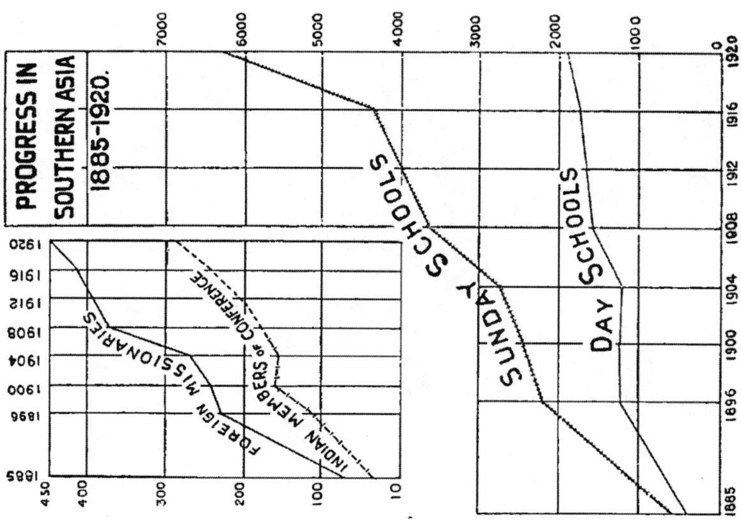
PROGRESS IN SOUTHERN ASIA 1885-1920.
SUNDAY SCHOOLS
DAY SCHOOLS
FOREIGN MISSIONARIES
INDIAN MEMBERS of CONFERENCE

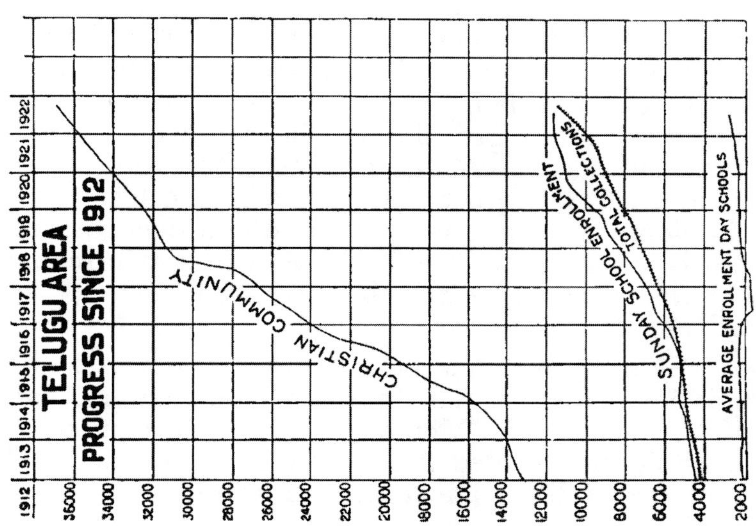
TELUGU AREA
PROGRESS SINCE 1912
CHRISTIAN COMMUNITY
SUNDAY SCHOOL ENROLLMENT
TOTAL COLLECTIONS
AVERAGE ENROLLMENT DAY SCHOOLS

Photo by F. C. Aldrich.

Bishop Warne baptizing a group of Chamars in the Meerut district.

community numbered fewer than 9,000. By that time the period of pioneering was over and the era of the mass movements had set in. By the beginning of 1900, Indian Methodism reported 111,654 as its total membership. Then came the period of the most rapid growth, for the following twenty years were to see the greatest advance that any Protestant Mission has ever had in the history of missionary operations. In these two decades, the Christian community of the Methodist Episcopal Church in Southern Asia rose from 111,654 to 421,646.

This wave rose most rapidly towards the middle of the second decade of this century, and if at that time the Methodist Episcopal Church as a whole had heeded the call of India,—if she had understood the statements and assurances of her leaders in India, and responded adequately with men and money, there is no question that Bishop Thoburn's prophecy would have been fulfilled in his lifetime and Episcopal Methodism in India have counted a million souls in its membership.

Photo by B. T. Badley.

The water buffalo in his " element,"—the muddier the water, the happier the buffalo!

What a record India has made in these past twenty years! What grounds for faith and encouragement she has given to the entire Church in her missionary endeavours! Consider the nature and extent of this success in view of the fact that for sixteen consecutive years, 1904-1920, our Church in Southern Asia added by baptism *annually* an average of 30,215 people, or a grand total of 483,447 baptisms in the sixteen years. The reports of the Annual Conferences give us at the end of 1922 a total Christian community of 421,646 people, and we expect to report at the Central Conference to be held in December of this year (1923) a total of about half a million.

Have "Mass Movements" Ceased?

Let no one suppose that Methodism's opportunity in India lies in the past. Great chances have indeed been lost, the harvest of the mass movements has only partially been gathered, but our greatest victories—if we will it so—are ahead. Here and there communities that have looked to us in vain have become disappointed, and their desire to enter the Kingdom has abated, but the voices of the thousands, calling us to " come over

Photo by B. T. Badley.

This man and his wife cannot read, but recently they became Christians, and now their son and daughter, taught in the Methodist school, read to their parents.

Photo by B. T. Badley.

A colporteur at home, looking over his stock of books before starting out on the day's work.

and help," are still in our ears, the hands of the multitudes continue to beckon to us, and we are still compelled, for lack of pastors and teachers, to refuse baptism to multiplied thousands. It is true that Christianity is not the only champion now of the "depressed" classes among whom these movements have taken place, but neither "reformed" Hinduism, which is so assiduously cultivating them, nor Mohommedanism, which is now bidding so widely for their allegiance, can do more than satisfy temporarily the deep desires and great needs of these millions. Social emancipation, economic uplift and educational advancement are, indeed, among their greatest needs, but these benefits can be based only on a spiritual regeneration that nothing except Christ's Gospel makes possible. The consciousness of this is certainly not well defined among these poor, ignorant and down-trodden masses, yet they have come to have a sense of this deeper need that no one has ever satisfied in the past or (outside of Christianity) seems able yet to meet.

Photo by B. T. Badley.

A potter making waterpots: his ancestors three thousand years ago were doing it in just the same way.

In the political upheaval that has followed the great war, India's outcastes have had to learn to their sorrow and amazement that "democracy," "self-determination" or "Swaraj" (Home Rule) are not to be the right of the outcaste, if the Brahman has his way! First dazzled, then dis-illusioned and finally despairing is the experience the sixty million poor and lowly outcastes have had during the past five years. Gandhi has been their greatest friend, and many other high caste Indians are standing for them. But even Gandhi, who so loudly championed their cause, has not pronounced against caste, as such, in Hinduism's social and religious structure, and his is, therefore, a half-way measure, already breaking down. Fifty years ago, the following paragraph, taken from a recent issue of a Calcutta daily paper, would have been unthinkable: to-day it creates no stir, and is tucked into a corner of the paper.

> "A significant movement is reported from the West Coast of Madras, where caste tyranny is more rampant than anywhere else in India. The so-called 'untouchables' of the Thiyya community who number about a quarter of a million, are now seriously thinking of changing their religion *en masse* in order to escape the tyranny of higher caste Hindus. It is hardly surprising when one learns that low caste people have lately been assaulted for daring to stand within a hundred yards of a West Coast Brahmin. At a recent Thiyya conference the president suggested that they should all become Buddhists, a proposal which is to be considered at a bigger conference. Meanwhile there have been many conversions to Christianity and to Mohomedanism, while missionaries of other creeds are busily endeavouring to capture this people in search of a religion."

This is not an isolated case. In many parts of India during recent months great conventions and conferences of various sections of the depressed classes have been held, to consider practical steps for securing economic and educational advancement, political opportunity and religious progress. Recently such a convention of Chamars (tanners, leather dressers and shoemakers by caste) met in the heart of one of our districts in the upper India field. There were eleven thou-

A great gathering of eleven thousand Chamars in upper India—met to discuss ways and means of elevating their community. The Christian message carried great conviction, and a new "mass movement" has begun.

sand of them at the meeting. Leaders of the neo-Hindu forces had learned of the gathering and their representatives were there in numbers, making their promises of help and pointing to new doors of opportunity to be opened to their "brethren." By invitation, some of our Methodist preachers were also present, and were asked to expound the principles of the Christian religion in its relation to the problems of the Chamar community. This they did with great effect, despite the fact that the Arya Samaj (the most aggressive of the neo-Hindu sects) leaders sought by every means to have the Christian preachers prevented from delivering their messages.

Photo by B. T. Badley.

A well of "compromise." The partition across the top keeps Hindus and Mohommedans separate, while they draw alike from the same water. India's logic is unique!

The outcome of the meeting was that the Chamars were most favorably impressed with the statements made by the Christians. A few weeks later this writer met the chief leader of the entire community of seekers, who said that his people were looking to every possible source of help for uplift and progress,—even to the political organisation of the Home Rule Movement, the National Congress. For himself, he had reached his final conclusion, which was that Christ alone could lift and save his community. This man, therefore, asked for baptism, with a view to seeking at once

Photo by B. T. Badley.

The oxen go down the inclined plane, drawing large leather buckets of water from the well at the top. A man at the well empties the buckets and throws them back for the return journey.

Photo by B. T. Badley.

A "Chaudhri" or headman of the Chamar caste from among whom Christianity has won so many disciples for Christ.

to lead his own people to take the same step and throw in their lot with the Christians. After two days of deliberation with him and the leaders of our Church in that district, he was baptized, and went forth at once with a holy earnestness to win his people. The latest report is that forty-six people of his community have just been baptised, and numbers of others are preparing for baptism.

Not only in upper India but in large sections of the South India field and in parts of the Bombay Area there are important movements among such masses of depressed people. Some of these mass movements have been going on for years and have brought thousands into the fold of our Church. The call is still for workers and funds to enable the Methodist Church to reap those great spiritual harvests. Caste, as a socio-religious system, must be abolished, and, with it, must go the social, educational and political advantages that the high castes have through the many centuries reserved for themselves. This is the only type of democracy that Christianity can stand for, and this is what the missionary advocates.

Who Is The Liberator?

Who is powerful enough to break this virtual serfdom that Hinduism has imposed on the mute millions in the past?—mute no longer in this new day of visions of enfranchisement and equal opportunity. Caste is going. " Untouchability " is doomed. Men are getting together. Humanity is asserting itself. Cleavages exist, but men are looking over them, and preparing to leap across them. A brotherhood is evolving, and it is being made on the lines of the Brotherhood of Man of which the Son of Man spoke. As the rising leaders of these sixty million outcastes scan the horizon, they see no one strong enough, or great enough, or good enough to set them free, save the living Christ. Some of their fetters have already been torn from them, while here and there can be seen the broken shackles of the past, but the hand that did this for them is a pierced one.

India's outcastes are watching just one great figure on the horizon,—it is Jesus Christ.

INDIAN METHODISM'S EPISCOPAL AREAS.

EPISCOPAL Areas as they now stand were organised in Methodism's India mission field after the General Conference of 1920, when this field came under the plan of the General Superintendency. The foreign mission field does not possess any more fruitful or remarkable territory than that contained in the four "Episcopal Areas" of the Methodist Episcopal Church in Southern Asia.

Without any further words of introduction, brief surveys of these Areas, furnished by the Resident Bishops, are given herewith.

THE LUCKNOW AREA.

Bishop Frank W. Warne, General Superintendent, Residence, Lucknow, U.P.

The Lucknow Area contains the original field occupied by the founder of the India Mission, Dr. William Butler, who started operations at Bareilly in 1856, and in 1858, after the Sepoy Mutiny had been quelled, made headquarters at Lucknow, the largest city of upper India with a population of nearly 300,000.

Geographically, the Lucknow Area includes a large part of the province of Bihar, all the United Provinces (including the hill districts of Garhwal and Kumaun, bordering on the closed lands of Tibet and Nepal), and the eastern part of the Punjab. This territory contains a population of some seventy-five millions. There are in it 68 towns and cities ranging in population from 15,000 to 300,000 in which the Methodist Episcopal Church has missionary work, including 64 educational institutions, aside from village schools of various types.

The Lucknow Area includes the most famous of the cities sought out by visitors and sight-seers from all parts of the world. These are Agra, Delhi, Lucknow, Cawnpore, Allahabad and Benares, in all of which save the last-named the Methodist Episcopal Church has important work. Our Church is not at work in Benares itself, but

The district superintendent of Pauri district on an evangelistic tour in the Himalayah mountains, following the famous pilgrim route to the Hindu temples among the snowy peaks.

Photo by B. T. Badley.

A view in the beautiful marble mosque of the Fort at Agra.

has important evangelistic work in its vicinity, where on account of the large mass movements towards Christianity among the Chamar community, many thousands of converts have been gathered during the past decade. This work is still young, but is full of promise for the future of our Church.

Allahabad, which stands at the junction of the Ganges and Jumna rivers, is the capital of the United Provinces. Here we have an English Church, for Europeans and Anglo-Indians, a Boarding School for boys and the district headquarters. It was at Allahabad that the Central Conference of Southern Asia was organised in 1885, and there also that the India Sunday School

Union of this field came into being in 1876 under the leadership of Dr. T. J. Scott of our Mission. Allahabad is one of the great " convention cities " of India, and a place of significance to Indian Methodism.

Cawnpore, the " Manchester of India," with its cotton and woollen mills and its tanning and leather works of many kinds, is the most important trade centre of inland India. Methodist activity there dates from the early seventies. It soon became a strong centre of " English " work, which is represented there now by an English Church and a flourishing High School for girls of European and Anglo-Indian parentage. The widely known " Lizzie Johnson Memorial Church " is the centre of a great work in the vernacular, supplemented by a Girls' as well as a Boys' Boarding School. In Methodist annals Cawnpore is noted

Photo by B. T. Badley.

Cutting hairs out of the nostril,—a wayside operation. The patient is not blind,—he prefers not to watch the point of the scissors!

Photo by B. T. Badley.

The window of the room in the fort at Agra where Shah Jahan, the builder of the Taj Mahal, was imprisoned by his son and not allowed to look on the Taj. When dying, he was carried out to the opposite side of the Fort and died gazing at the Taj.

for its strong and aggressive group of Indian laymen, well-to-do financially, and during the years of the past making Cawnpore probably the greatest centre of lay activity in our Indian Church.

The city of Agra, made world-famous by its unsurpassed " dream in marble," the Taj Mahal, has long been a seat of Methodist operations. An English Church was maintained by us there for many years, but for lack of a missionary pastor has had to be closed for the present. The city is the centre of important evangelistic operations which, with the help of the urgently needed men and money, can be made of supreme importance.

Delhi, the capital of the Indian Empire, is also the headquarters of one of Methodism's great districts in India. For many years now it has been the centre of one of our greatest mass movements in this field,—a work that calls urgently for reinforcements. There are now more than 27,000 in our Christian community in the district. Delhi is to have the " Butler Memorial," a building to enshrine the memory of the great founder of the work of the Methodist Episcopal Church in India. Plans are also under way for suitable institutions, in which the Woman's Foreign Missionary Society is taking a prominent part.

This brings us, in our list of cities, back to Lucknow, the Episcopal headquarters for the Area, and world famous for the great defence of the " Residency " in 1857 under Lawrence, Havelock and Colin Campbell. This is one of Methodism's great centres of missionary operations in Asia. The two Colleges maintained by our Church in the Southern Asia field, the Lucknow Christian College for men and the Isabella Thoburn College for women, are both located at Lucknow. In connection with these there is a High School for girls

Photo by F. C. Aldrich.

A man of God,—veteran preacher in the North-west, winner of souls and exemplar of the "higher" life.

and a Middle School for boys, both with the finest hostel accommodations attached. Here also is the great and flourishing Methodist Publishing House of the city, which has had an unsurpassed financial record during the more than sixty years of its existence. This Press publishes millions of pages of religious literature annually in five languages, and also prints the official organ of this field, "The Indian Witness," one of the leading Christian weeklies of India. Other periodicals are also printed here, including the "Kaukab-i-Hind," (Star of India), Sunday School lesson leaflets and

Children's papers.

Lucknow has also one of our leading English Churches, the first to be established by us in India, and ever since a centre of spiritual influence which, through the annual "Dasehra Meetings" for the deepening of the spiritual life, has widened so as to touch almost every part of our field, and make Lucknow a spiritual nerve centre in Indian Methodism.

This completes the list of cities of note, as the sight-seer might decide, but omits mention of a large number of strategic centres in the work of the Kingdom. Reference must be made at least to some of these.

Photo by B. T. Badley.

The terraced hillsides of the Himalayahs produce both wheat and rice, as well as varieties of small grain. The fields are, on the average, about ten to fifteen feet wide.

Photo by F. C. Aldrich.

This man dug down the mud shrine in the village and then about forty people were baptized in that ward.

First, there is Bareilly, the first station to be occupied by Methodism in India, boasting the first orphanage and school to be established by us in India, as well as the first Theological Seminary, and also the first Hospital for women, to which in 1870 came Clara Swain, the first lady doctor in India. All three of these institutions still are among the largest and most successful in this field, all doing a notable work for Indian Methodism. The latest institution to come is the Bareilly Baby Fold, where already modern facilities are provided for the care of more than twenty babies and children under the supervision of an American lady missionary and her assistants.

Meerut must also be mentioned, the seat of a Girls' High School, a Boys' Middle School and the centre of the greatest mass movement our Church has ever known. What has happened within a radius of twenty miles of Meerut during the past thirty years, beginning under the leadership of the great P. M. Buck, makes one of the most glowing chapters in the annals of Methodism. These great movements both among the Sweepers and the Chamars have given Meerut district, though divided and re-divided on account of its growth, the largest Christian community of any district of our Church in India,—35,000.

Other cities such as Muttra, Aligarh, Budaun, Moradabad, Shahjahanpur, Sitapur, Hardoi, Bijnor, Roorkee, Muzaffarpur and Gonda are full of interest, whose history brings up such great names in Methodist annals as Bishop J. M. Thoburn, Bishop E. W. Parker, J. L. Humphrey,

Photo by B. T. Badley.

Distributing temperance and other tracts among the jute workers of the Home Mission field, Bhabua, Bihar.

T. J. Scott, B. H. Badley, J. H. Messmore„ J. W. Waugh, Robert Hoskins, J. C. Butcher and others.

Space will permit of special reference to only one more city, *viz.*, Naini Tal. This is one of our stations in the "hills,"—the great Himalaya

Photo by L. A. Core.

Mohommedans of Budaun celebrating the great Mohurram festival.

mountains. Naini Tal boasts the first house of worship built by Methodism in India, now more than 60 years ago. Its cool climate early made it the leading health resort of North India, and here our Church in the seventies established a sanitarium for its missionaries. Early in the eighties it erected a beautiful English Church, following on the establishment of schools for missionary children and the children of the domiciled community. Thus " Wellesley " and " Philander Smith College " began their record-making career, and represent to-day the highest type of institutions for English-speaking boys and girls in this land,—an inestimable boon to missionary children for more than 40 years. A High School for Indian boys followed in due time, with a strong Hindustani Church. To-day Naini Tal fills a place in the Lucknow Area of prime importance.

But with this enumeration of the cities of the Area, mention has not been made even of all the district headquarters, there being twenty-eight districts in the Area with a total missionary force of 40 men and 39 women. The Christian community of 242,700 is rapidly increasing, the growth being held up only for lack of sufficient pastoral supervision and educational facilities for the boys and girls of the communities that might be baptised. Missionary hearts have been breaking in the Lucknow Area because of the necessity of refusing baptism, year after year, to many thousands who knock for admission at the doors of our Church. And still the multitudes wait. And still our cry continues to be—" How Long?"

The Lucknow Area has an old and established work in every line of missionary effort, with a growing body of educated Indian laymen and ministers. In self-support the Area has gone beyond all expectations, the amount raised last year in benevolent and all other collections totalling Rs. 1,17,330, an increase of 67 per cent. over the previous year. Its educational institutions are unsurpassed, its plant and equipment are more and more becoming adequate to our needs. Its young people crowd the schools and churches, while vast non-Christian populations are accessible as never before to the message of Christ. Here the

Children of the Baby Fold for Upper India. One of the most popular institutions in the Area, started at Bareilly two years ago, has already outgrown its premises.

Woman's Foreign Missionary Society has a most successful and expanding work. Our present successes have been built upon great achievements in the past, but the future is full of promise of still greater triumphs. With a reasonable support continued from the Home Base while we still further develop our own resources in men and money on the field, and especially with a still greater outpouring of God's mighty spirit upon us, we shall move forward to the greater victories of the new day.

Photo by M. T. Titus.

Scene at a bathing festival on the banks of a "sacred" stream in upper India.

THE BOMBAY AREA

Bishop J. W. Robinson, General Superintendent,
Residence, Colaba, Bombay.

IN the terminology of the Methodist Episcopal Church this name is applied to that work of the Church found in Baluchistan, Sindh, Rajputana, the Punjab, the Bombay Presidency, Central India, the Central Provinces and the Berars. It has an area of about 825,000 square miles and a population of approximately 87,000,000 people. As a matter of easy comparison, the Area is equal to fifteen states of Iowa, and its people would fill forty Iowas to the present density of the population of that State.

As compared with some other parts of the work of the Church in India that in this Area is comparatively new, and we can in no wise be said to occupy the territory of the four conferences which comprise it. Rather, these furnish the outline we are trying to fill in. Many other missions are co-operating in the effort to evangelize this mass of people, but as perhaps the largest, and certainly the mission with the most widely diffused work, the heaviest burden of responsibility for the evangelization of the Area falls upon us.

But while the work is comparatively new in most parts of the Area, rather remarkable results have been attained. At the close of the last year our statistical report showed we had 2,097 organized Sunday schools with a total of 73,306 registered attendants; 451 Epworth League chapters with a membership of 11,905; 470 day schools of all grades with 13,066 pupils, and ministerial support and benevolent collections for the year amounted to Rs. 1,30,071. During the year there had been 10,546 baptisms, and the Christian community claiming relationship to the Methodist Episcopal Church totalled 107,025. Compared with the as yet untouched masses, these figures are very insignificant, but when compared with the difficulties we meet they are almost startling, and

Photo by O. M. Auner.

The Training School for village workers, Khandwa, Central Provinces, is "on the job." Twenty thousand enquirers in that district wait while these five men, and their wives, secure their training.

Photo by J. T. Perkins.

A missionary "Ford" crossing the Mainganga river, Central Provinces, on four hollowed-out logs.

prove that the leaven of the Kingdom is beginning to work among the people. And the moral and spiritual effects of this leavening, not to be indicated in any statistics yet devised, are far more significant than those we report in figures.

As is inevitable in a field the size of this Area, there is great diversity in the work. Pioneering on our frontiers covers much territory and absorbs a considerable amount of our effort. Some of this pioneering is in the heart of the jungles of Central India, and is largely among Animistic tribes. In the jungle stations of Baihar, Jagdalpur and Sironcha we are in touch with the great Gond people, and touch as well tribes that are yet more primitive. The response of these peoples in the centres named and their out-stations is most encouraging. We hold it incumbent on missionary

Photo by B. T. Badley.

The date palm, showing the vessel near the top of the trunk for catching the juice that exudes from the gash made in the trunk at the point where the branches start. The lower part of the trunk shows the wounds of previous years.

statesmanship to see that these aboriginees are given the Gospel before they are absorbed in the enveloping Hinduism or won by the aggressive Mohommedanism that seeks them.

An entirely different kind of pioneering is that involved in the work along the northwestern frontier. Afghanistan is a forbidden country to both Christians and Christian work, but we are camped at its very door, and yearly touch and teach thousands of its Mohommedan tribesmen who come down from the rich Kandahar Valley with their caravan loads of fruits for shipment from Chaman to the great cities of India. The spiritual life of Mohommedanism is as sterile as the countries it occupies, and work among them is almost as forbidding as are the desert wastes of this

Photo by A. N. Warner.

The temple at Ramtek, Central Provinces. Low caste people are not allowed to approach too near the temple. Democracy!

frontier. But in Chaman, within two miles of the border, there is now an organized Church, with about a hundred and twenty-five members, and even the Pathan from across in Afghanistan is compelled occasionally to feel something of the influence and beauty of this spiritual oasis in a desert of fanaticism. In the Quetta Valley we are opening up several centres, and while the people

Photo by S. Aldis.

A Waterfall in the Central Provinces.

as a whole are not friendly, we do find the few that welcome us. Our workers at times follow the military railway westwards the entire breadth of Baluchistan and even into East Persia, and there have been baptisms in several places, including the line's terminus, Duzdap, Persia. At this latter place, as well as at Chaman, numerous caravans converge from all Central Asia, and we look forward to the time when the generosity of some

Photo by Mrs. J. T. Perkins.

Tiger shooting is not in the missionary line, but occasionally even a missionary will "bag" a tiger.

friend of man will enable us to establish hospitals and evangelistic work at both places to an extent that will enable the merchants and travellers of these caravans to take back to their distant homes and countries an adequate impression of the things for which Christianity stands. As seed-sowing places what better centres can be found than these frontier outposts!

We have two large and fruitful mass movement areas. Gujarat, one of the garden spots of India, began to yield its fruit to us about twenty-five years ago, and in that conference we now have one of the best bits of mission work in the land. Sunday school work and village schools are particularly good, and the average of collections for pastoral and benevolent purposes is perhaps higher here than among any of our other large communities in rural sections. While the crest of the mass movement wave has perhaps passed, there is a steady stream that is encouraging. In the east of this conference we are developing a splendid work among the Bhils, an aboriginal tribe, and there has also begun a movement among caste people that has brought in several hundred converts. This latter movement is arousing severe persecution.

Photo by B. T. Badley.

A wayside "ophthalmic optician," able to test eyes, fit spectacles,—and, at the same time, ruin your eyesight!

Photo by B. T. Badley.

Schoolboys of the Methodist school for boys at Raipur, Central Provinces, acting a scene in an original play featuring the king of the beasts.

The Punjab is our most fruitful field, and the physical stamina of the people, their industry and keenness to acquire homes in the newly opened irrigated regions, their liberality in giving, their zeal in propagating their new religion, and their general attractiveness, give promise of splendid future extensive and intensive development. Rajputana and most parts of the Central Provinces and Bombay conference territories are as yet resistant. Here our converts are not coming by the households and castes, but by the ones and the twos. But the field is being prepared by faithful work, and in due time the harvest will begin, as has been the case in the past in our now fertile fields.

Our seaport cities furnish at once our most difficult and our most important fields of effort. "Bombay the Beautiful," with its more than a million and a quarter of people, and Karachi, the grain port of the northwest, are within our borders, and up to the present we have done comparatively little to impress on their cosmopolitan crowds the message which Methodism has for men. However, we see a change in prospect. In Bombay, with the aid the Centenary has been able to promise us, we are maturing plans that will enable us to take our rightful place among the Christian forces that are working for the welfare of the city.

Photo by F. Wood.

Modern tenement houses, similar to these, are being erected in great numbers in Bombay to meet the need of the rapidly increasing number of mill hands and other workmen in the city.

The remodelling of the old Grant Road Church now nearing completion, gives us an evangelistic and social centre in a very crowded part of the city, while sufficient funds are in sight to enable us to begin the development of a second centre at Sankli Street, a most strategic location, which will provide

Photo by A. N. Warner.

A great religious fair of the Hindus in the Central Provinces. The outcastes are segregated on the near side of the sacred lake.

a church home for two vernacular congregations, school and workmen's hostels, offices for church workers, residence for two missionary families, rooms for missionaries departing and landing, and other facilities for a really aggressive work. No doubt in due time Karachi will be able to take a like forward step.

The human key to all our work is the Indian worker. For too many years we were content to employ for our Church's agents the cast-offs of

The re-modelled and enlarged Church at Jubbulpore for the use of the English-speaking community.

other missions. We rejoice that day is now past. Aside from district training institutes for local workers, we now have Bible Training or Theological schools for our Hindi people at Jubbulpore, for our Marathi people at Nagpur, for our Gujarati people at Baroda, for our Rajputana and South Punjab people at Ajmere, and for our frontier people at Quetta. For our better educated ministers of all India a Methodist Theological College, which gives instruction in English, has been established at Jubbulpore. These all need to be strengthened, and with their improvement will come a great strengthening of the entire work.

Photo by Dr. C. I. Kipp.

Bishop Robinson and the Chief Commissioner inspecting the Mary Wilson Sanatorium at Tilaunia, Rajputana.

THE CALCUTTA AREA.*

Bishop F. B. Fisher, General Superintendent, Residence, 3, Middleton Street, Calcutta.

READING his episcopal address at the Central Conference of Southern Asia held in 1900 at Calcutta, Bishop Thoburn said: "This city is geographically nearer the centre of the vast territory which we occupy than any other important town which can be named. Calcutta will probably continue to be the metropolis of Southern Asia for at least a century to come."

This statement of Bishop Thoburn's regarding Calcutta applies still more to the Southern Asia field as it now is, with Malaysia and the Philippine Islands detached. The metropolitan nature of the Calcutta Area is still more apparent from the fact that it contains two of the five great port cities of India, the second being Rangoon. In the early days, Bengal and Burma were linked together to make an annual Conference; to-day they are united to make the Calcutta Area.

---

*NOTE:—Burma is not covered by this survey as a separate booklet is to be issued for that field.

Not only is Calcutta the metropolis of India, but towards it are setting the great tides of population. Any study of the situation will show that the movement of the races in the Southern part of Asia is from the northwest to the southeast, from Persia, Mesopotamia, Afghanistan, the Punjab and Upper and Central India towards Bengal and Burma. Some of these lines of movement terminate with the coal and iron fields around Asansol, others end with the city of Calcutta itself with its population of more than a million inhabitants, (1,327,547 according to the census of 1921), while others pass through Calcutta down into the wonderfully rich and fertile fields of Burma and the

Photo by B. T. Badley.

The house in the background is the birthplace of the novelist, W. M. Thackeray (1811), Free School Street, Calcutta.

Malay Peninsula. This is what has made Rangoon already largely an Indian city, whose Indian merchants represent the most wealthy community there. This also has made Calcutta the greatest centre of Hindustani-speaking people in the Indian Empire, there being in it, according to the government census, 464,756 people " born outside of Bengal," which number, with their families unable to be thus classified, would bring the number well over the half million mark. " There is not a province of India with fewer than 1,000 representatives here, and one of them (Bihar) has 264,222, while another (the United Provinces) has

Photo by B. T. Badley.

A typical Chamar,—tanner and shoemaker caste: photographed in Calcutta where, with thousands like him, he works, going back to his home occasionally " up north."

Photo by B. T. Badley.

Unique work in Calcutta,—a meeting with Christian sweepers who live on top of one of the great department stores of the city.

127,217." The great majority of these people speak Hindustani.

But population, industries, trade and commerce are not Bengal's only claim to greatness. It is true, in a special sense, that Bengal has been, from the time when the West first touched the East, the leader of thought and progress among the provinces of India. Her people have, on the whole, more culture, a completer system of education, a larger number of newspapers and a higher position in India's social, political, intellectual and spiritual world than those of any other province. The earliest reformers, educators, scientists and patriots were from Bengal. All this tends to assign Calcutta the leading place in Indian thought and life, and gives to its future the promise of still greater importance.

Calcutta was discovered to Methodism by William Taylor, who, in 1870, amid difficulties almost inconceivable now, organised our first Church; it was made great in Methodist annals by that peerless leader, administrator, prophet and seer of Indian Methodism, Bishop James M. Thoburn. These great souls left a permanent impress on the city and were followed by such great workers and builders as David H. Lee, Bishop J. E. Robinson and Bishop Frank W. Warne. To their sagacity, devotion and tireless energy as well as to the wisdom, faith and courage

Photo by B. T. Badley.

Rural Bengal is dotted with these picturesque little Hindu temples.

Photo by B. T. Badley.

Sprinkling "holy" water on a goat before the priest (standing at the right in the picture) strikes off its head with his big, curved knife: scene at Kalighat temple, Calcutta.

of those who followed them, we owe the possession of one of the most remarkable plants for missionary purposes that any Church holds in the city. The spiritual centre is Thoburn Church on Dharamtala Street at its busiest and most valuable point. Here too are located the Parsonage, the great Calcutta Girls' High School and the residence for the missionaries at work among the women of the city. Further down Dharamtala Street, on the east side of Wellington Square, stands the far-famed Lee Memorial Mission with its superb plant, accommodating a school for Bengali girls, a Normal School and Kindergarten, and furnishing the centre for a wide-spread work of evangelism among the Bengali women of the city. Still further along Dharamtala Street is the large building now to be occupied by the Collins Institute, an important high school for boys, with a hostel attached for the Christian students. A little further along this great thoroughfare is the centre for evangelistic work among men, both Bengali and Hindustani. Here is to be erected our new Central Church, on a site unsurpassed for the purpose in the city. South from this site, on Corporation Street, is the Calcutta Boys' High School with its large and valuable property. At Beliaghatta the Lee Memorial Mission maintains an educational and evangelistic centre of great importance, while on Tangra Road are located the hostel for our Bengali Christian boys and a missionary residence for the district superintendent of the Bengali work. In addition there are several centres for vernacular evangelistic work.

A prominent layman of Thoburn Church has turned over to our Mission a large property with a going concern, valued at $200,000, to be used as a "Goodwill" industries plant. This promises success to our Church in a new sphere of effort.

The property most recently acquired is at No. 3, Middleton Street, which is probably the choicest site ever obtained by the Methodist Episcopal Church in any city of India. This is in the best residence section of Calcutta, not far from the "maidan" (the great park of the city) and looking out towards the wonderful "Victoria Memorial." On this site is a commodious building of three storeys, accommodating the episcopal residence, the residence and offices of the General Treasurer of the Board of Foreign Missions for Southern Asia, as also for the Central Treasurer of the Woman's Foreign Missionary Society for this field, and furnishing headquarters for the Executive Secretary of the Centenary Forward Movement of India and Burma. Additional space is rented.

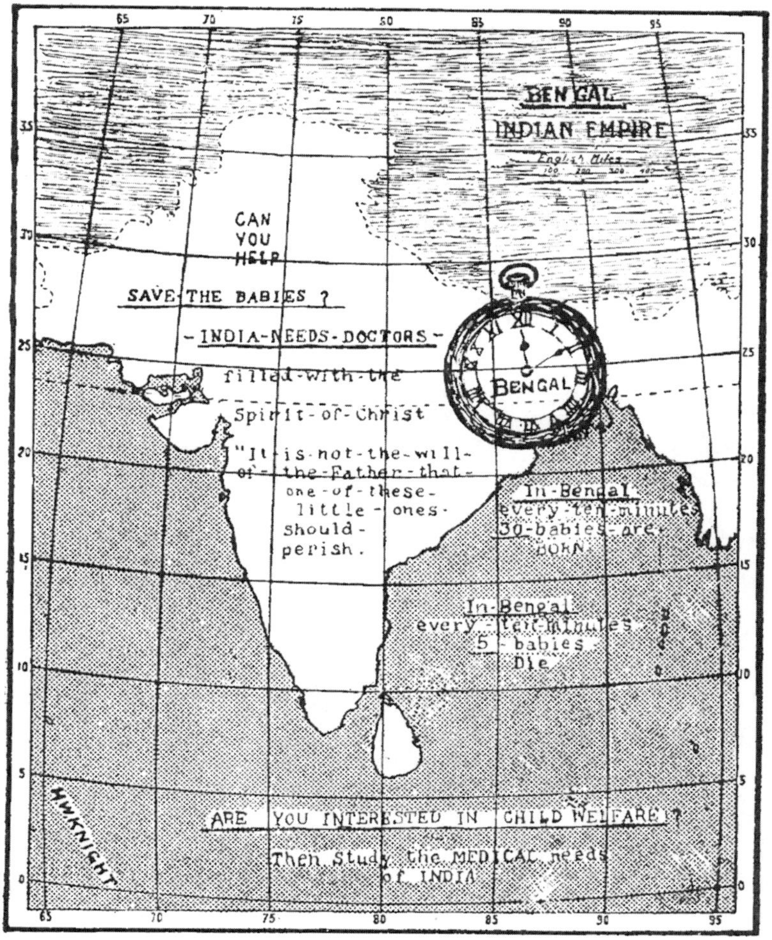

In Bengal every ten minutes thirty babies are born, and every ten minutes five of them die. Yet some people claim that India offers no field for medical service!

This property affords an ideal site for the proposed American Church, which will care for the spiritual interests of the large and growing community of American business men in the city, and doubtless afford a Church home for the many European business and professional men holding membership in various Free Churches whose needs are not met by the other Churches in Calcutta. The erection of such a Church and the securing of the right man as its pastor are imperatively needed if the spiritual welfare and progress of this large and increasing community are to be assured. Calcutta presents no greater immediate need or opportunity.

But Calcutta is not the only centre where marked success has been achieved in the matter of

Photo by B. T. Badley.

The Banyan tree, with its aerial roots, is characteristic of Bengal. Missionary work in the villages has an unending charm.

securing valuable and suitable property. One of the most signal undertakings of the Area is in Darjeeling, where we have recently acquired the hill-top property now known as " Mount Hermon," and where the foundations are being laid of the new Queen's Hill School for daughters of mis-

Photo by Pearl Madder.

Bishop Fisher signing the cheque on one of the boundary pillars of "Mount Hermon," Darjeeling, thus closing the deal that brought that property to the Bengal Conference.

sionaries and girls of European and Anglo-Indian parentage. This site comprises 60 acres of the choicest land that the Himalaya mountains contain, adjacent to Darjeeling, and every foot of it high and looking out across the great mountains and valleys to the wonderful peak of Kinchinjunga,

28,000 feet high, and to the long line of unbroken snowy grandeur running for scores of miles along the horizon and hiding behind them that monarch of the world's majesties,—Mount Everest.

The Calcutta Area has always been a stronghold of " English " work. The foreign born and Anglo-Indian community has always been large, and it was among these classes that Methodism secured its initial successes. Thoburn Church, with its great auditorium, ministers to hundreds and is a spiritual power-house in the metropolis. Plans for the American Church have already been referred to, and Asansol, where we have maintained an English Church for many years, is another centre where an American Church might be organised, to provide spiritual shepherding for the Americans who are increasingly finding employment in the great coal and iron mines, and especially in the factories in that region which are introducing American experts, machinery and methods. Our Church has carried its share in the Union Church at Darjeeling for English-speaking

These furnaces at Asansol, built by American engineers, have replaced the older types.

Iron castings in the Asansol district: foundries are able to turn out single pieces up to twenty-five tons each.

people, and ministers to small congregations elsewhere.

The wonderful industrial development in and around Asansol is forcing new opportunities and problems on us, and emphasizing in a new way the relation of the Church to the entire industrial problem of modern India. Some idea of the industrial wealth and expansion of that region may be gained from the statement that there is more iron ore to be had there than in the entire continent of Europe. Coal is being mined in great quantities, and the industrial development in that region has made that section of Bengal the greatest industrial centre in India. In the heart of it all Methodism has long been planted and is in a position to lead the forces that make for spiritual life.

Evangelistic work in rural Bengal has never yet attained to very large proportions. Even the oldest Missions have reaped meagre harvests in the villages. The time seems to be coming when

A modern plant in the Asansol iron region, built on American lines.

Iron Railway sleepers are turned out at the rate of 1,200 tons a week. Indian Christian men and women labour in large numbers in the industrial region of Asansol, and are much in demand.

this will no longer be the case. The beginnings of mass movements among the Santals have already resulted in hundreds of baptisms and, with the necessary equipment, our Church might be the leader in gathering the entire Santal community into the Church. Near Gomoh also a spiritual work of great promise has started, leading to many baptisms and clearly indicating that the masses have begun to move there.

This is the situation in which the Methodist Episcopal Church finds itself at work in Bengal. The morale of the Bengal Conference was never so satisfactory as to-dav. A high grade ministry,

Photo by B. T. Badley.

The American tractor at Dr. Rabindranath Tagore's farm (near Bolpur, Bengal) being explained to interested villagers by the Indian operator, a graduate of Cornell, New York.

with a strong and educated body of laymen, are at last available for the great forward movement that has almost everywhere begun. So many young men of education and promise have joined the conference within the past two years, and the attitude of our student community towards Christian service has recently undergone so marked change, that the common thought of the conference membership, whether missionary or Indian, is summed up in the expression—A New Era.

Photo by B. T. Badley.

The Victoria Memorial at Calcutta, erected at a cost of ten million Rupees, to the memory of Britain's greatest Queen. Three-fourths of the money was raised by popular subscription.

The Calcutta Area, facing unprecedented opportunities to-day, and vibrant with new life and energy, yet realises that the passing centuries have not changed the hope of humanity, and exclaims with the prophet of old—" Not by might nor by power, but by My Spirit, saith the Lord of Hosts."

THE BANGALORE AREA.

Bishop H. Lester Smith, General Superintendent, Residence, Bangalore.

THE South India Annual Conference which forms the Bangalore Area includes all that part of India lying south of the Bombay, Bengal and Central Provinces Conferences. It includes all of the great Madras Presidency, a part of the Bombay Presidency, and the States of Hyderabad and Mysore, the two largest native states of India.

The general shape of the Conference is that of a great triangle with an area of 170,000 square miles. Within the Conference limits live 57,207,000 people, most of whom speak one of the four great Dravidian tongues, Telugu, Tamil, Kanarese, and Malayalam, although there are many Hindustani people in the cities and some Marathi folk in the north and north-west.

This population is roughly divided into the following religious groups :—

Hindus	50,727,000
Mohommedans	3,910,000
Roman Catholics and Syrian Christians	1,550,000
Protestants	910,000
And others	110,000

Of this great population the Methodist Episcopal Church is responsible for the evangelization of 11,433,000. At this present moment we have won to faith in Jesus Christ a total of 67,899, which is just about one in every 168. In other words, we have won less than 6/10 of one per cent. of those for whom we are responsible and who will die without Christ unless we evangelize them.

Photo by Bishop H. Lester Smith.

Boys of the Methodist school at Vikarabad, Deccan, preparing a kiln of lime for burning.

In addition to the overwhelming mass of non-Christians still to be reached, the problem of evangelizing this host of unevangelized is made unusually difficult by the language barriers or divisions. The multiplicity of languages in the Conference requires the duplication of schools and other institutions for training and the provision of a separate staff of workers for each language area.

Photo by Bishop H. Lester Smith.

A class of young people received into the Church at Kolar on "Children's Day" this year.

An excessive number of missionaries and trained workers is thus absorbed in educational and training institutions and a larger body of workers is required than would be necessary in single language conferences.

We do work in a large way in the Conference in English, Telugu, Kanarese and Tamil and have some work in Hindustani.

A third feature of the Area which increases the difficulty of the task is the scattered character of our work. Belgaum, Bangalore and Madras and Yellandu Districts are removed by distance ranging from 250 miles to 700 miles from the rest of the field. This fact further accentuates and increases the necessity for a duplication of institutions and missionary staff, since it is very difficult indeed to educate and train our workers at such great distances from their homes, even where the language barrier is not present, except in the case of the higher grade workers.

These general difficulties and many others more local in character, confronted the missionaries of the Conference as they met in Joint Session for the Post Centenary Survey.

The upper class of the Beynon-Smith High School, Belgaum, on the occasion of the arrival of a new missionary Principal.

Photo by Bishop H. Lester Smith.

A boy of our industrial school at Bidar, Deccan, inlaying silver on articles of gun metal.

The entire missionary task of the Conference was thoroughly examined and all possible phases of the work carefully considered in both committee and conference sessions. A few general conclusions were reached which will be of interest to the Church, I am sure.

In our educational work it was decided that our minimum goal should be as follows :—

First, we must have a High School for both boys and girls in each language area. In no other way can we possibly train leaders for our work and properly care for our Christian community.

Our present equipment is as follows :—

We have two English High Schools in Bangalore which are both doing thoroughly good work. We have a fine Girls' High School in the

Telugu area at Hyderabad and, a little more than a year ago, organized our Telugu Boys' High School at the same place. This new school is having a phenomenal growth in numbers, has already been recognized temporarily by the Government and will be permanently recognized as soon as the buildings, now under construction or contemplated, are completed.

We have a fine Kanarese Boys' High School at Belgaum and have already made good progress in our plans for a Girls' High School in the same place.

We have not yet been able to make even a beginning upon our Tamil High Schools.

Pupils of a primary school in a village of the Belgaum district.

Our program for Middle Schools provided for about double the number we have. Of these two are building: the Girls' Middle School at Raichur and the Boys' Middle School at Madras. A third has been planned at Tuticorin for the boys. Land

Photo by Bishop H. Lester Smith.

Articles of gun metal with silver inlaid, manufactured by Methodist boys at Bidar, Deccan.

has been purchased but building has not been begun yet. It is thought possible to have the Tuticorin School take both boys and girls for the primary and early middle grades and the experiment will be carefully watched and carried as far as possible. In some of the other Missions in the South, co-educational Middle and High Schools are thoroughly satisfactory. The development of our other Middle Schools must await money and staff.

Our training requirements are sadly incomplete. We desperately need double the number of training schools for village workers and at least two higher institutions. At Kolar we have the building for a good training school just completed and we hope it will soon be in operation. At Hyderabad the Bible Training Institute needs more money for building and staff to make it really function in the Telugu area.

Our industrial educational program is prosperous at Kolar. At Bidar and Gokak Falls we have started work which promises well. With sufficient means, we can have a fine work established at each point, but at present the money is lacking.

The Medical work of the Conference is in better condition than a year ago. The Woman's

The industrial plant at Gokak Falls, in the bounds of the South India Conference, where the Methodist Church has an important work along modern lines.

Foreign Missionary Society hospital at Kolar has been re-opened and is doing fine work. The General Hospital at Vikarabad is flourishing. The hospital at Bidar is being repaired, refurnished

"Bible Readers" of the South India Conference, typical of the splendid force maintained in India by the Woman's Foreign Missionary Society.

and will soon be re-opened. In all the hospitals however, more especially at Vikarabad and at Bidar, there is still need for more equipment and a more adequate staff.

The evangelistic work of the entire Conference is sadly undermanned in all departments. There is a critical shortage in both men and women missionaries and a serious lack of Indian workers. The serious character of this shortage may be appreciated from the single fact that we are absolutely unable to teach and train our converts as fast as we have received them. We are now working

Photo by Bishop H. Lester Smith.

Children of the "Baby Fold" maintained by the Woman's Foreign Missionary Society at Kolar, Mysore.

against overwhelming odds in an endeavour to speed up our work so that we can catch up with the rate of increase.

In conclusion however I would say that everybody is happy and joyously full of faith and courage. We have abundant reasons for thanksgiving. We have had splendid additions to our property and equipment which are either completed or are provided for in the appropriations of either the Board of Foreign Missions or the Woman's Foreign Missionary Society, or both of them, at Hyderabad, Bidar, Vikarabad, Raichur, Kolar, Belgaum, Madras and Tuticorin. We thank God for these and take courage to believe that in due time our other necessities will be provided.

In the second place the work is going with a splendidly victorious swing. We have mass movements in every language area which are abundant evidences of the presence and blessing of the Holy Spirit.

Photo by Mrs. H. Lester Smith.

The first village of Lambadis baptized recently by Bishop H. Lester Smith: the beginning of a most hopeful movement.

This very year we have had an unusual movement of this kind among certain caste people, the Lambadis, in the Gulbarga District. The Lambadis of this district are agriculturists, and own their own lands and are a fairly prosperous and substantial community. They have had regular instruction for several years and finally several villages asked for baptism. When I was touring through the villages of the Deccan in January and February of this year, I examined them carefully, and finding them qualified, I baptized five villages with their headmen, about 330 souls in all. Other villages are now seeking baptism, and as fast as we can train workers we will baptize them. These people are fully able to pay for their own schools and preachers. They are a recognized caste having the right to use the caste well, etc., and will be a valuable opportunity for the reaching of others in the caste groups.

South India Conference rejoices in the glorious and victorious progress of the work of the Kingdom of God. Though there be difficulties and though there be tremendous obstacles, we are not downhearted. " Jesus shall reign where'er the sun—Does his successive journeys run."

" This is the victory that overcometh the world—even your Faith."

We believe in Christ, we press forward in holy confidence to His final triumph.

THE LAND OF THE HUNDRED-FOLD PLUS.

IF Jesus Christ had started out on the day of His baptism to visit all the villages of India, and had gone to one every day from that time till now, He would still have before Him 48,205 villages unreached. So some one has estimated. There are three-quarters of a million villages in India; figure it out.

No wonder, then, that evangelism is taken by our Church to be the supreme issue in India. And, of course, our missionaries have gone to the villages. It is in the rural areas that the Church has grown most rapidly in this land. In the past ten years, Christianity has gathered in about a million converts, almost all from the villages. It is the work of evangelism in the little towns and surrounding hamlets that will account for the great growth of Christianity in India. The increase, according to the decennial census made by the government, shows that while the total population of the country has increased 1·2 per cent. during the past decade, the growth of the Christian community has been at the rate of 22·65 per cent. This is many times more rapid a growth than that of either Hinduism or Mohommedanism. The statistics of the government as to the Christian community are always about 10 per cent. lower on the average than those of the Churches, for the enumerators in the government census are always non-Christians, and they bring pressure and persecution to bear on the poor and almost illiterate Christians of the villages, in order to keep the numbers of Christians as low as possible in the census. The growth of the Christian community in India during the past decade, according to the statistics of the Missions, would show at least a 25 per cent. increase.

The Secret of Sacrificial Service.

Evangelism is the watchword of a militant and victorious Church. Many leaders among the

Photo by B. T. Badley.

A typical scene in bazaar preaching in an upper India town. Religion is always the most interesting subject in an Indian crowd.

Hindus are asking,—" How can we adapt Hinduism to modern conditions, so as to make it meet the needs of a new India based on the ideals of democracy and social progress?" Thinking men among the Mohommedans are raising a similar question,—" How can we interpret Islam so as to meet the requirements of the progressive new age, and keep our faith vital in the midst of conditions so different from those that existed when the Koran was written?" These are pertinent questions, but religions that have to ask them and are compelled to make adjustments of such a serious nature, can of course have no time or strength for the real missionary task. We rejoice that our Christ is adequate to, abreast of, sufficient for and master in every situation that has ever developed in the world. With Him as our leader, our great question is not " How shall we save the Church?" but " How can the Church save India, save the world?"

It is this consciousness of the unchanging truth of the Gospel of Christ, and this knowledge of the inherent superiority of its principles to those of any other religion whatever, that gives to the Christian missionary an invincible faith. This brings the knowledge that there is a *message* for India in the Bible which must be given and will be accepted. The missionary in India has no doubt as to the sufficiency of the Gospel or the power of Christ. This is what leads to a willingness on the part of thousands of missionaries to pour their lives out for India in sacrificial service.

Listen to Dr. Howard Somervell, who last year accompanied the Mount Everest party as the doctor in charge. He said recently at a meeting of the London Missionary Society at Westminster, when offering himself for service in India :—" *En route* for South India immediately after the Everest climb, I found a district containing a million souls, with only one doctor to look after them. I took ten days' duty for the overworked doctor, and what I saw during those ten days of appalling need changed the whole course of my life. I know all the catchwords about 'dear brethren,' 'darkness,' and so on, but the sight of the people themselves was very different. I could do nothing else." What Dr. Somervell did not see from Mount Everest, he saw clearly on the plane of India's desperate need. He was appointed as a medical missionary to Travancore.

Aggressive Evangelism.

For many years now the Methodist Episcopal Church in India has had a Commission on Aggressive Evangelism, and this has kept the entire Church stirred up on this question of supreme importance. It has also arranged each year for a month of special evangelistic effort by our Church in every part of the field. The report of this special campaign month for this year has just been published, and some idea of the extent and significance of this work can be gained from a summary of the report :—

Number of meetings held ...	44,156
Number present ...	1,163,702
Total baptisms ...	9,738
Gospel portions sold ...	81,134
Tracts distributed ...	919,633
Idolatrous shrines destroyed ...	675
Number of laymen helping ...	5,089
Number of days given by laymen ...	7,882

If all the results could be tabulated, these figures would be considerably increased, but even so, they indicate something of the magnitude of the campaign. And who can estimate the direct and indirect results that cannot be reduced to figures?

Photo by Dr. Sarah Vrooman.

The Kali Ganga River, shown on the left, for more than 100 miles, separates Nepal (on the left) from British India. Dr. Martha Sheldon's grave, near Dharchula, is at the mountain's curve beyond the clump of trees.

Photo by Dr. Sarah Vrooman.

The Snows of Tibet on the left: Snows of Nepal on the right. In the foreground is Bhot, British India. Methodism was represented in this region by the late Miss Martha Sheldon.

A New Chapter.

Some years ago the need and opportunity for special evangelistic work among the educated classes became so apparent that the Rev. Dr. E. Stanley Jones was given his whole time to develop this particular kind of work throughout this field. For four years now he has devoted himself to this task and has succeeded in opening up a unique type of work. No missionary in India has ever before had such a wide hearing on the part of the educated classes. The students and professors of the great university centres, the professional and business men in the cities, Hindu and Mohommedan leaders in social and political reform movements, and the large and growing cultured classes of the land have responded in a wonderful way to the opportunities given them through Dr. Jones' addresses and sermons to hear the Christian message interpreted to them in the light of new India and in view of their national and individual needs. The messages given by Dr. Jones throughout the great centres of India have been constructive, sympathetic and brought down to the level of India's everyday need in the realm of the social, moral and spiritual. They have had as a background a broad knowledge of what is best as well as that which is weak in the great religions of India, and the personality of the speaker has been invested to the full in this effort to win India's intellect for Christ. Dr. Jones' ministry has been so markedly successful that it may be considered to have opened a new chapter in the approach of Christianity to the educated classes of this land. Some detailed reference to it will be of interest and bring encouragement to all who are working to bring in Christ's kingdom.

" The most significant movement is not the mass movement in the villages," says Dr. E. Stanley Jones, " it is the mass movement in mind toward the Christian position. He who gets the thinking of a people will sooner or later get the people. Christ is capturing the thinking of India to-day." He goes on to say :—

" Nine years ago Dr. John R. Mott addressed a large gathering in the Victoria Hall in Madras. In the midst of the address he used the name of Christ and was hissed by the audience. This year in the same hall we had six nights upon one topic alone—Christ. The hall was filled and the last

This man, who with his family was baptized a year ago, has already been instrumental in bringing about fifty-five baptisms in the Rae-Bareli district.

nights packed, and for an aftermeeting several hundred Hindus publicly stayed for prayer, and to find peace of mind and heart through Christ." Of another place he says: "The students of the Hindu College asked for a special address for them, and when asked what subject they wanted, replied—'We want you to tell your personal religious experience.' These students put off a cricket match to come to a lecture on Christ."

Hindu Tributes to Christ.

Dr. Jones has found the political leaders equally interested in the life of Christ and the story of His crucifixion. He writes: "Last Easter time the organ of the Non-Co-operation Movement, the paper of which Mr. Gandhi was editor, published about four columns of matter for four weeks on the death of Jesus."

Dr. J. H. Oldham of the "International Review of Missions" was talking with Mr. Gandhi and Mr. Natarajan, when the latter said: "Well, Dr. Oldham, it is very difficult for us to say where our Hinduism ends and our Christianity begins." After quoting this, Dr. Jones relates the following:

"I was lecturing in Bombay, and the editor of the 'Indian Social Reformer' was the chairman of the meeting. In his closing remarks he said:—'I suppose the epitome of what the speaker has said is this,—that the solution of the problems of the day depends upon the application of the spirit and thought of Jesus to those problems. I am not a Christian, and you will be surprised to hear me say that I entirely agree with these conclusions.' He went from there to preside at the All-India Social Conference. This man is probably the greatest thinker on social affairs in India, and he sees no way out but the Christ way."

" A chief judge," continues Dr. Jones, " of one of the Native States (a Hindu) said to one of our audiences :—' If to be like Jesus Christ is what it means to be a Christian, I hope we will all be Christians in our lives.' "

On another occasion Dr. Jones was lecturing at the great new Hindu University at Benares, and a Hindu professor in introducing him said: " I have been attending these public lectures, and my chief interest was in the personality concerning whom the lecturer was speaking. Young men, no other such personality as Jesus Christ has ever appeared in human history. I repeat it, Jesus Christ is the greatest character that

Photo by B. T. Badley.

A fine specimen of the " sacred " Pipal tree (ficus religiosa). The Hindus build shrines at the foot of many such trees: note the worshipper in this case.

has ever appeared in our world. And we can begin this spring festival in no better way than to hear more about Him."

Christ, Reformer, and Regenerator.

" I know of no reform, whether in the moral, social, religious, economic or political realm,—if it be a reform and not a re-action—that is not tending straight towards the Christian position," declares Dr. Jones. In line with this he tells how on one occasion the Hindus and Mohommedans of Palwal were going to have a public debate on the question of which religion makes men most moral. They both agreed, beforehand, to leave out Christianity from the discussion, " for," said they, " Christianity is head and shoulders above us both." He tells also how a Mohommedan student, in giving his address in the closing exercises of his college, said: " We must study the Bible. There are many things in our religions that need correction, and we must correct them by the Bible." Then Dr. Jones adds: " Jesus has changed the whole moral and spiritual atmosphere. He is forcing modification everywhere. But He stands unmodified. We have had to modify nothing in regard to Him in the clash of things in India."

" Some non-Christian lawyers," relates Dr. Jones, " were having a banquet in north India. At the close they were being entertained by a professional entertainer who made the company rock with laughter as he mocked the old gods and told funny stories about them. He then began to mock Jesus Christ. A silence fell upon the company. The silence turned to resentment, and then they angrily hissed him off the stage. They could laugh at the old gods, but not at Jesus Christ." What a commentary is this on the new situation in

India, or this other that Dr. Jones gives: "A life of Gandhi, put out by Hindus, is filled with references to Jesus Christ on nearly every page, and yet, as far as I remember, not a reference to Krishna or Buddha is to be found in it."

Can Hinduism be "revived?"

All these things speak of a new India and show that India's attitude towards Christ and the Bible has undergone a far-reaching and fundamental change within recent years. But we cannot yet claim that the attitude in India regarding the Church has changed. It is in process of changing, however, not only because India is learning to value in it what meets her deepest need, but also because she is beginning to discount what is merely a temporary phase in its form or methods. At the same time the Church itself is consciously seeking to make such adjustments in its organisation and affiliations as are necessary to bring it more into harmony with national ideals.

Side by side with all this distinct gain on the part of the Christian Church, there have been steady disintegrating forces at work against Hinduism. No one can deny that there has been a real revival of Hinduism in recent years, but the outcome of this revival is beginning to be perceived, by Hinduism itself, even if but dimly yet, is not what had been hoped. Regarding this Dr. E. Stanley Jones has a very pertinent word:—

"A revival is a good thing if the system is based on ultimate spiritual and social facts, but it may be its undoing if it is not. It is extremely doubtful if Hinduism can stand a revival. Dr. Farquhar says: 'The revival of Hinduism has been accompanied by a steady inner decay.'"

But whether Hinduism should undergo successfully a complete re-adjustment to modern thought and conditions or not, there is lacking in it the drawing power of Christianity. This is because Hinduism, with many incrustations of philosophy and speculation, theories and ideals, has no dominant personality to hold the heart of mankind. "I was talking with a gentleman of real discernment," says Dr. E. Stanley Jones, "and asked him what he thought of Jesus Christ. 'Well,' said he, 'there seems to be no one else seriously bidding for the heart of the world except Jesus Christ. There is no one else on the field.'"

How true it is that aside from Jesus Christ, humanity knows no one who universally draws the heart of man. How well India has shown the truth of Christ's own words,—"And I, if I be lifted up, will draw all men unto me." Listen to the words of a Hindu professor, speaking as chairman of one of Dr. E. Stanley Jones' meetings at Allahabad :—"The thing that strikes me about Jesus Christ is His imaginative sympathy. He seemed to enter into the experiences of men and feel with them. He felt the darkness of the blind, the leprosy of the leper, the degradation of the poor, the loneliness of the rich and the guilt of the sinner. And who shall we say He is? He called Himself the Son of Man, and also the Son of God. We must leave it at that."

Blind "Globe-trotters."

And yet there are people in Christian countries,—apparently well informed and certainly well educated people, who profess and seem to believe that the impact of Christianity on India is negligible. Visitors to this country rush through the land seeing the "sights" in the great cities.

avoiding missionaries, ignoring Churches, Christian schools, colleges, hospitals—institutions of all kinds—not taking the time to talk with people on the field who could give them correct information, —and then rush back to England or America and announce with the utmost assurance that Christian missions in India amount to nothing, that they themselves have been there and *know*, that they went through all the great cities and saw nothing of the work or people that the missionary reports tell about! It is absurd, and still more so that many are ready to believe such talk. " It is rather amusing, if not pathetic," says Dr. E. Stanley Jones, " to read an article in the 'New York Times' by an American engineer, who spent five years in India, saying that ' Christianity is utterly without

Photo by B. T. Badley.

Weaving blankets in a town of north India.

influence among the Indian people to-day.' He was a delegate to the special session of the Indian National Congress at Calcutta in 1920, called to discuss the question of passive resistance. The very movement amid which he sat had its inspiration from Christian teaching, for Mr. Gandhi said to the writer in an interview,—'I got my idea of passive resistance from Matthew 5 : 38, 39. It was the New Testament that fixed it in my mind.' When Mrs. Sorojini Naidu, the great nationalist lecturer and poetess, sent a poem to the National Congress to be read, she chose for her title a verse of Christian Scripture: 'By love serve one another.' "

India's Best Known Book.

The statement is not too strong, that among those who can read in India the Bible is the best known book. It is also true that it is acknowledged to contain the standards by which men are judged. The most ardent defenders of Hinduism or Mohommedanism seek, at best, to prove that their religious books are *as good* as the Christian Scriptures, and that their spiritual guides are as worthy as the Christ. The effort is never made to show that they have a superior book or greater personality than has Christianity. The standards, it is commonly acknowledged, are set by the Gospel; perfection of character is reached in Christ. When the Non-Co-operators wished to compare Gandhi with the highest and best, they did not turn to Buddha, they did not think of Mohommed, they did not quote Krishna,—they spoke of Gandhi as being like Christ! His trial was compared to the trial of Christ, his imprisonment to the crucifixion of Christ. Millions have gone so far as to claim that he is an *incarnation* of Christ!

The sales and distribution of the Bible, and especially of the New Testament and the Gospel portions, have gone far beyond anything in the past. This interest in the printed word is showing itself all over India by the way in which the non-Christian newspapers quote the Bible, freely use its allusions, and even expect their readers to be familiar with its personages and ideals.

Newspaper Evangelism.

This has made it possible for our Centenary Movement to start a far-reaching work of newspaper evangelism. Brief Christian messages are inserted in about a dozen of the leading non-Christian papers and magazines. These messages give, in unqualified terms, the most definite Christian teaching, unhesitatingly claiming for Christ the supreme place as both Teacher and Saviour, and setting forth the New Testament as the one guide and ideal for India in this great day. Not only are these advertisements gladly accepted, the space being paid for at current rates (though several papers have made special concessions owing to our " noble purpose," as one editor put it), but other Hindu and Mohommedan papers, seeing our messages, have written, enquiring if they too may not carry these in their columns. Meantime, a steady correspondence has resulted, giving the Executive Secretary of the Centenary Movement an unprecedented opportunity of getting and keeping in touch with earnest souls all over this land. The yearning and heart-hunger on the part of educated Indian young men thus revealed, makes one long to have his entire time to follow up this type of personal work for the Master.

EXPERIENCE IS FINAL PROOF.

Science can solve some of our problems, but not all. There is a realm in both the physical and the spiritual world where nothing short of personal experience can satisfy us.

Chemistry can tell us the constituents of water, but the way to know whether or not it will quench thirst is to try it. Proper analysis may correctly tell us of what material the rice grain is formed, but the way to know if it is a health-giving food is to try it.

The philosophies of the various religions may tell us much about them, but the way to determine whether or not they satisfy the human heart is to try them and see. **The Bible says:**

"BELIEVE ON THE LORD JESUS CHRIST AND THOU SHALT BE SAVED."

Is this true? **Try it and see.**

THE MOST POWERFUL PERSONALITY.

The Vice-Chancellor of one of the great Universities of India, speaking recently before a large body of Indian students of all religions, said :—

"If you ask what is the **Most** Powerful Influence that has entered my life to shape it. I will tell you that it is THE BIBLE."

This man is a Hindu. What influenced him in the Bible was not history, biography, poetry or prophecy, but a living personality—Jesus Christ.

Study the Bible and find Christ.

Christ's Voice
AND
India's Destiny.

A leading Hindu journalist says :—

"Many eminent non-Christians turn for guidance in the perplexing problems of national life to the teachings of Christ. India earnestly hopes that the great body of Christian missionaries in this land will stand by her in her endeavour to apply the central teachings of Christ to her national life."

The teachings of Jesus Christ are found in the New Testament, in whose pages He speaks a message for all men. When India hears His voice she will attain her destiny.

Centenary Forward Movement,
3, Middleton Street, CALCUTTA.

INDIA NEEDS REST.

Jesus Says :—

"Come unto me all ye that labour and are heavy laden, and I will give you rest."

India needs rest,-peace of heart and mind. Christ's invitation is to India, and He says :—

"My peace I give unto you, not as the world giveth give I unto you. Let not your heart be troubled."

No sincere or earnest seeker will be disappointed, if he will take the **New Testament** as his guide. In those pages, somewhere, he will meet the living **CHRIST.**

Centenary Forward Movement,
3, Middleton St., CALCUTTA.

WHO IS JESUS CHRIST?

People ask "Who was Buddha?" "Who was Akbar?" "Who was Napoleon?" But they always ask "Who *is* Jesus Christ?" The difference in the tense used is significant.

Christ is not a memory or a historic figure. He is a living personality in our world to-day. He touches the lives of people everywhere. His transforming power is all around us.

Christ can never be classified as a mere man, nor as a super-man. He is the Saviour of Mankind. Study the New Testament and the truth of this will appear.

Centenary Forward Movement,
3, Middleton Street, Calcutta.

Western Civilisation or Christianity?

Many people in India seem to think that for India to accept Christianity is to adopt Western civilisation. Such a view is not merely shallow but is wholly mistaken.

Christianity has given to the West whatever of lasting worth it possesses, but Western nations cannot trace to Christ all their institutions or practices. Indeed, many of these are directly opposed to the spirit of Christ.

India is being offered and is in a position to study pure Christianity, without Western accretions.

India's hope, individual and national, lies in accepting Christ.

Centenary Forward Movement,
3, Middleton St., CALCUTTA

Samples of Messages used in Centenary Newspaper Evangelism.

India is not only responding to the appeal of Christ but is accepting Him as teacher, guide and Lord. The land is full of disciples of His who are not yet ready to break with caste and sacrifice property and social position. "When a man can stay in his home and be a Christian," says Dr. E. Stanley Jones, "then the task of Christianizing India will be simplified. A Hindu said to the writer: 'When that day comes, it will be easy for Christianity.' Holland (the Rev. W. E. S.) gives this illuminating incident: He overheard two Hindu students arguing the question of caste.

The Rev. G. Gershom (on the right), district superintendent of the Belgaum district, with the workers of one circuit.

One argued that it was a good thing. The other turned to him in surprise and said: 'But you say that,—you who are progressive in your ideas?' 'Yes,' replied the other, 'I do, for caste is the last trench we are holding against Christianity. You know yourself that if it were not for caste, practically every student in this hostel would be Christian before morning.' "

Surely India is on the eve of coming out and accepting Christ. The millions are not ready yet to receive baptism or join the Church, but they are considering the step. Let us close by referring to some very striking meetings that Dr. E. Stanley Jones conducted in South India recently. He writes:

> "I had series of meetings for educated non-Christians in various places. I had felt for some time that I ought to try a new method in dealing with them. At T. we had large crowds of non-Christians out, probably a thousand each night. The last night I put this up to them: 'I will leave the question of baptism to your consciences, but will you here and now accept Jesus Christ as your Lord and Master, openly and before all, and will you begin a Christian life? I asked those who would do this to stay at the close and meet me in a room at the back. T. is a very orthodox Hindu city and I wondered how many of them would do it. I expected four or five to respond. To my surprise I found a hundred Hindus there. I told them how to accept Christ, how to put the habits of prayer and Bible study and service into their lives. I asked them to repeat a prayer of confession and surrender after me sentence by sentence. They did so. A few months before the whole city was stirred over the baptism of a girl, and here were a hundred Hindus openly and frankly accepting Christ as their Saviour and Lord. Out of this number I do not know how many will be baptised. We have formed a class of them to help them live the new life. A Christian judge is taking the class."

Photo by E. M. Moffatt.

The famous Hindu temple at Kidarnath in the snowy range extending between Garhwal and Tibet.

This remarkable meeting was followed by another equally so at R........... A meeting of the Non-Co-operators was going on at the same time, which Dr. Jones had been asked to address but had decided not to, as it was his last evening in the place and he wished to have an after-meeting. He says:

> "In spite of the other meeting going on, we had the hall packed again, and in response to my invitation to surrender to Christ we had about forty of the finest men in the audience stay for the after-meeting: some of these were lawyers and other substantial business men. How many of these will ultimately be baptised I do not know, but it was fine to see them publicly take their stand for Christ."

"The Kingdom is coming,—O tell ye the story." We are telling it, and there is great joy in our hearts. The same Christ is our leader who has led and triumphed among the nations, and He will not fail nor be discouraged, for He is to reign!

The Outcastes' Exodus

By Bishop F. B. Fisher.

They come, the men of sorrows come;
Along the toilers' dusty road,
Forsaking superstition's load,
Escaping slavehood's bitter goad,
In faith they come.

They come! the care-worn women come;
From out the hovel's prison door,
The smoke-stained walls and mud-dung floor,
Bowed down in grief and sorrow sore,
In hope they come.

They come! the naked children come;
Already weary, having toiled,
But eager, hopeful, bright, unspoiled,
Though born in squalor, souls unsoiled,
They, child-like, come.

They come! the waking millions come;
They see the cross where Jesus died,
Behold the wound-print in His side,
They turn to follow this dear Guide,
Redeemed, they come.

They come! who greets them as they come?
Shall sons of God, touched from above,
Like palsied priests, unworthy prove?
Oh, let us rise in Christ's great love,
And *bid* them come!

MANY things have recently happened in India, and many more are yet to come to pass. The reaction of the national political situation on the life and activities of the Christian Church have not yet been satisfactorily estimated, for they are not yet fully understood.

Some things, however, are clear and among them this, that a radical adjustment must be made in the realm of authority and control. A larger measure of autonomy must be provided for this field of Methodism's life and effort and for other " foreign " fields.

This does not mean that Indian Methodism wishes to become independent of the Home Base. It may be possible to find, here and there, an Indian radical who would stand for complete separation and autonomy, but this does not represent the situation, either as to the missionary element or our Indian leaders.

What is " The Next Step?"

With regard to the further development of the Methodist Episcopal Church on the foreign fields the question has been raised as to whether our goal should be national Churches independent of the American Church, or a world-wide Church with organic unity assured. This issue has been joined particularly by the publication of Dr. Paul Hutchinson's "The Next Step" and Bishop Neely's "The Methodist Episcopal Church and its Foreign Missions." Various articles on the subject have appeared, and, as General Conference draws nearer, the number of such articles will probably increase. The subject is already on the "Agenda" for the forthcoming Central Conference on this field, and unquestionably this will be among the important questions to which the General Conference of 1924 will have to give a clear reply.

It should not be wondered at that the "foreign" fields are not content to remain "foreign" permanently. As long as they are just this, they are merely appendages to some distant ecclesiastical organization which has its "Base" at "Home," and controls by a long arm of authority. In the beginning of things this was not only inevitable but desirable, but as a permanent plan of action it was sure to raise, as it has raised, difficulties.

Despite such a re-actionary book as Bishop Neely's, one can sense throughout Methodism a definite opposition to the breaking up of an organic Methodist Episcopal Church by the formation of independent units based on national lines. Some have taken satisfaction in the course adopted by Japan when she became "independent," but the precedent is not suited to the needs of the Church as a whole. There is, however, no alternative to the course adopted by Japan, unless the Constitution and practices of the Methodist Episcopal Church can be so modified as to permit to growing

What principles will govern Methodism in her international polity as she deals with the new India?

national fields a life of self-expression and control consonant with their development.

In other words, Methodism in India has reached a stage when the share she has had in shaping her own course during the past no longer suffices, and, indeed, is no longer in keeping with her welfare and dignity. Even the increase of the powers of the Central Conference granted by action of the General Conference of 1920 will not suffice. This should not be surprising when it is remembered that in the supreme legislative body of the Church the representation of our Southern Asia field representing a Christian constituency of more than half a million, was in the proportion of one to forty in the 1920 General Conference. Moreover, in a body constituted and conducted as is our General Conference, meeting in a land on the other side of the world, a foreign field must undergo severe disadvantages, in addition to the utter inadequacy of its numerical representation. As a matter of fact, a very small percentage of any foreign delegation ever gains the floor of a General Conference. This is not reflecting on the men who have represented Southern Asia, or any other foreign field, and doubtless their personal influence and their voice in committees and sub-committees had weight, but no field can be content with such a subordinate place as this. This is true especially in view of the great issues involved, for it is the General Conference that legislates for the Church, determines what is to go into our book of "Discipline," elects our Bishops, shapes our polity and settles all the major matters that can come up for decision by the Church.

India Not Ultra Radical.

In India this question has taken on very large importance because of the great national movement which has now gone into every part of this land and is destined to result in due time in the establishment of Home Rule. This is the ambition of all political parties, and this is the plan and intention of the British Government. The influences of this new national consciousness and purpose have vitally affected the Church in India, bringing in the time when new and definite steps towards self-determination for the Indian Church must be taken. Conservatives in America, or in India itself, may regret this, but there can be no doubt that General Conference will be faced with the question of granting a larger measure of autonomy to the major foreign fields,—certainly to India.

A few opinions from some of our well known Indian men in the various Areas are here given, that we may have their own voice in this matter.

"Autonomy in the Indian Church is a two-sided affair. The Church at the Home Base should be prepared to transfer as much authority to the Indian Church as the latter can take over. This devolution cannot be immediate, but it must keep pace with the growth and development of indigenous leadership. The final goal should be to make the Indian Church independent of foreign resources of men and money. The relation of the foreign missionaries should be that of *leaders and advisers* and not that of *masters and directors*, so that the Indian Christians shall be trained and prepared by them for autonomy. To be self-centred and unwilling to trust capable Indian Christians with positions of responsibility will be suicidal to the entire missionary work.

On the other hand the Indian Christians should not so much *claim* as *deserve* autonomy. They should be increasingly aggressive in assuming the financial and administrative responsibility of their Church. I, for one, feel that we cannot honorably claim a voice in Church matters unless and until we shoulder the burden of responsibility. To this end the need of an educated, trained and consecrated ministry and laity is most imperative, for autonomy in the hands of any other kind will kill the Church. There is sufficient evidence that the Indian Church is ready for a larger measure of autonomy."

J. R. CHITAMBAR.

"In my opinion the time has come when Indian Christians of proved worth should be given a larger share of responsibility in our Church. From an economic point of view, this will be a sound policy, as in the Indian field a large number of missionary recruits involving a much higher salary, furlough and other allowances, will not be necessary. Again, the missionaries who come from their home-land will have sufficient time to learn the language and to enter sympathetically into the various problems of the Church. I do not find fault with the appointment of raw missionary recruits from the homeland as District Superintendents, as I quite realize that in making certain appointments no other choice was left. But I do hope that experiments will be made from now with available Indian men of ability, by giving them at least posts of District Superintendents, wherever possible."

L. B. CHATTERJI.

"This is a day when people want their own leaders over them. The Church ought to awake and get ready for what is going to come. Responsible positions have to be opened right away to Indians in order to encourage them to carry on the work by themselves. If the Indian heart is to be captured to work for a self-supporting and self-propagating Church, a large measure of autonomy must at all costs be given. The people will then see the whole work of the mission in a different light and will support the work in a better way than they are doing at present. We do not want a *foreign Church*, but desire to build up a Church that is purely Indian with indigenous management and leadership."

O. DAVID.

(1) *Rev. D. M. Butler*, Chandausi (2) *Rev. Yusuf Dhanji*, Baroda (3) *Rev. Robt. John*, Bulandshahr (4) *Rev. J. Devadasan*, Bareilly (5) *Rev. & Mrs. J. R. Chitambar*, Lucknow (6) *Rev. G. L. Lorenzo*, Lucknow (7) *Rev. L. B. Chatterji*, Calcutta (8) *Rev. Emmanuel Sukh*, Buxar (9) *Rev. G. Gershom*, *Belgaum*.

" I am in favour of a larger share of autonomy for those Churches in Indian Methodism which are in a fair self-supporting condition, or whose spiritual life and activity can be gauged by the Christian Stewardship principle. For such Churches, and only for such, self-determination can be a blessing."

A. LUKE.

" Methodism in India has given her children a larger measure of autonomy than any other Church in India has hitherto done : and yet she could do more. The time has come when the number of missionaries must decrease and Indians should be given a larger measure of responsibility and freedom. Experiments in that line have proved that confidence placed by missionaries in certain Indian leaders has not been in vain."

S. K. MONDOL

" The national consciousness pervading Indian political life is not unnoticeable in the Church. There is a growing demand for Indian ways and methods of worship and for ecclesiastical self-determination. Methodism in India has passed the stage of being reckoned in terms of a Mission and Mission workers. These are signs betokening need of autonomy in the Church, and the power of future Indian Methodism depends on the speed and wisdom with which it accommodates itself to the spirit of the times."

MORRIS A. PHILLIPS.

" With all my national aspirations for a complete self-determination in all matters political, I am rather conservative in matters ecclesiastical. Considering seriously the condition of the Indian Methodist community—its lack of capacity for establishing itself as a Church, its lack of assuming any form of independent responsibility, and the lack of spiritually-minded intellect and leadership—I, for the present, do not believe in any larger measure of autonomy in Church administration than what it now enjoys."

M. C. SINGH.

"Autonomy must be brought about, and the starting point is the local Churches. These must have autonomy in finance, management of their affairs and choice of pastors. Provision should be made for a general Board of (local) Churches. At present, evangelism, Church management and conferences are 'missionary-centric.' We can't be ruled from beyond the seas."

DHANJI FAQIR CHAND.

"Considering the question from all points of view, I have come to the conclusion that self-determination in the near future should be our aim. It is but natural. Too much interference on the part of parents leads the grown up children to revolt; but parental advice and guidance in solving deep problems will always be welcome and beneficial."

A. RAHIM.

Note:—A number of others were asked to contribute to this symposium, but, for one reason or another, failed to do so.

These sentiments, with varying shades of opinion, represent the younger generation of our Indian leaders in the India of to-day, and the probabilities are that such feelings will gain strength and find new expression as the years go by. The cry ten years ago used to be,—"We don't wish to be controlled by the missionaries!" That was the individual speaking out, showing the growing spirit of personal independence. Now it is the educated group within the Indian Church speaking, and their demand is,—"The Indian Church must not be governed, its policies determined and its Bishops appointed from across the seas!" A few years hence, the rank and file will become articulate, demanding self-determination within the Church. For the present, conservative elements are still markedly evident. But the problem is before us, and the Methodist Episcopal Church in India is demanding a solution.

Is India "foreign" in a World-wide Church?

If Indian Methodism must pay the price in order to stay within the fold of the Methodist Episcopal Church, so must American Methodism pay the price if she wishes to retain organic union with the great and growing branches of the Church in this "foreign" field. In the first place, why should such a field be "foreign?" If there is to be one great Church, why is India more "foreign" than America? To the Indians, America is very "foreign,"—hopelessly so! Can we not have a world-wide Church, in which each nation takes its rightful place, contributing its full and peculiar

An Indian District Superintendent, the Rev. P. D. Phillips of Bijnor, starting out in the mission oxcart on a round of quarterly conferences. There are now sixteen Indian Superintendents on this field, which is 25% of the total. Their number is steadily increasing.

share to the whole, and helping to mould the life and destinies of the one common Church? Bishop Neely in his recent book replies definitely in the negative. It is not conceivable that in this attitude he represents the thinking of American Methodism. India would rather believe that Bishop Bashford voiced the thought of our Church when he pleaded against breaking up Methodism into separate national units, each going its own way. Bishop Neely vigorously opposes the notion (voiced by our Bishops resident in Asia) that there is a " rapid development of our Methodist Episcopal Church into a world-wide organization." He maintains that if this were the case, it would lead to disaster for our Church, and holds that a " world Church " is undesirable and dangerous, that it could not exist and continue to maintain true democratic principles, but would become an ecclesiastical autocracy such as we have in the Roman Church to-day and would menace the independence of Methodism in America. If Bishop Neely is correct in this conclusion, or if this should be the real thought of the General Conference of our Church, there can be no question but that India must ultimately seek separation from the Methodist Episcopal Church. If things are to continue as they now stand, there is not a sufficiently good outlook for the rising generation of Indian patriots who are beginning to assert themselves. They have no quarrel with the past, but the future cannot be shaped according to it.

The Ultimate Issue,—Leadership.

The crux of the matter is reached in the issue of leadership. It would prove our Church in India hopelessly dead if, at the time of the great national awakening, when the entire land is preparing for and moving towards Home Rule, the Church should be indifferent in the matters of independence and self-determination.

It is the success of the past that has brought our Church in India to the strength and vision which now make possible a vitality and self-expression that tell of life and hope. In this supreme hour in India, it is only India's sons and daughters who can bring about the greatest things. They need help, they require guidance, but they are the really potential agents in this situation. The hope of the Church must, more and more, be in them. They do not wish to get rid of the foreign missionaries: they realise that for many years to come, a support from outside will be necessary, but they do not think that this fact

Photo by B. T. Badley.

Preaching and distributing Christian tracts in the new Home Mission field, Bhabua, Bihar.

should interfere with the supremely important cause of bringing into existence as rapidly as possible a strong, self-supporting, self-propagating and, only then, self-respecting Church.

Recent years have tended to make for strained relations between Indians and foreigners in this land, but in the Methodist Episcopal Church in India the ties of sympathy and understanding have been strengthened. The splendid spirit that has characterised the relationship between Indian Christian leaders and foreign missionaries in our Church will become still more marked as together we toil and pray for the coming of the Kingdom.

The Church of the Brotherhood.

Some may think that the Church in India is to be purely Indian. Why should this Church be established along racial lines? Will its membership be restricted to people of Indian birth? Will the foreign missionary be a mere spectator? This is not the hope entertained by Indian Methodism. The Church in India must have the best that India affords, plus the finest that any other land that loves her can bring. These two elements, blended by love and in service for the Motherland, will together serve the Church in India,—a Church not controlled from without but moulded from within.

The Church in India is looking for a new world wherein dwelleth brotherhood. On India's broad plains, and beneath her bright skies, there is being fashioned the brotherhood of the new world, —made on the pattern furnished by the Son of Man. He Himself is helping us to bring it into being and shape it in strength and beauty. He is the greatest on India's horizon: He is supreme on the horizon of the world.